CONNECTI

PRAYER

JOSEPH L. HUSS

Dr. Joseph L. Huss
Growth Publishing Company
1300 NE 56th St., Unit 57190
Des Moines, IA 50317
www.josephhuss.com

ISBN: 979-8-9891623-0-7
Printed in the United States of America

CONTENTS

Introduction

"What a privilege to carry everything to God in prayer"[1] run the words of an old and beloved hymn. Do we fully appreciate this privilege? Do we understand that God wants and even longs for us to pray? Through the prophet Jeremiah, He extended an invitation and a promise: "Call unto me, and I will answer thee, and shew thee great and mighty things, which thou knowest not" (Jeremiah 33:3). In the New Testament, God prompted the Apostle Paul to write, "Be careful [anxious or troubled] for nothing; but in every thing by prayer and supplication with thanksgiving let your requests be made known unto God" (Philippians 4:6). Yes, God wants us to pray, and He has done everything possible to encourage us to pray.

We as God's children have a direct and open line of communication to the Creator of the universe. When we come to Him in prayer, we will never get a busy signal or be sent to voicemail. He always has time for all of us. Because of Christ's sacrifice for us on the cross, we must "come boldly unto the throne of grace, that we may obtain mercy, and find grace to help in time of need" (Hebrews 4:16).

Although I count it a privilege to pray, I also count it a privilege to share with you what the Bible has to say about prayer. My hope and prayer is that this book will help you put scriptural concepts of prayer into daily practice, as well as bring you into a closer relationship with God.

> *O magnify the LORD with me, and let us exalt his name together. I sought the LORD, and he heard me, and delivered me from all my fears. . . . O taste and see that the LORD is good: blessed is the man that trusteth in him. Psalm 34:3-4,8*

1

"We can obey God
without loving Him,
but we cannot love God
without obeying Him."

A Relationship with God

The very title of this chapter could be startling to many in the world today. A relationship with God? Most people believe that He is out there – somewhere – but they wonder, "Is He involved in the goings-on of this world?" Does He really care about what happens down here, and does He specifically care about me?

The simple answer is yes.

> *For God so loved the world, that he gave his only begotten Son, that whosoever believeth in him should not perish, but have everlasting life. John 3:16*

God loves the world and everyone in it, and He has made a way for every person in this world to have a personal relationship with Him. When you have a relationship with God, He gives you ever-lasting life as a gift: life that can begin right now and never end.

Prayer - Connecting with God

But there is only one Way, and His name is Jesus. He is God's only begotten Son, and He said, "I am the way, the truth, and the life: no man cometh unto the Father, but by me" (John 14:6). If you do not know God personally, it is important that you pay earnest attention to this chapter. For if you do not have a relationship with God, you cannot apply what the Bible says about prayer to your life. This chapter is the foundation to everything else written in this book.

In any relationship, communication is the most important element. By definition, a relationship involves a two-way transfer of information between the parties. If there is no communication, there is no relationship.

In a relationship with God, communication is just as important. God communicates with us through His Word and through the Holy Spirit. How do we communicate with God? We communicate with God through prayer.

Although prayer is a commonly understood concept, Christians generally do not pray as if communicating with God were that important or special. If we were to poll a group of believers and ask them, "Do you think you pray as much as you should?" the vast majority would very likely respond, "No." Most of us have at least a vague feeling that our prayer lives are somehow lacking. We know in our hearts that our communication with God is not what it could be.

Our lives are filled with tasks that need to be done soon and tasks that should have been done a while ago. Unfortunately and to our own detriment, our minds are so cluttered that we feel we cannot take the time to get away and talk with God. In our pursuit of the seemingly urgent, it is too easy to lose sight of what's really important.

In prayer as in all other things, we should allow the Lord Jesus Christ to be our example. The Scriptures clearly show that He took time to be alone and pray.

> *And when he had sent the multitudes away, he went up into a mountain apart to pray: and when the evening was come, he was there alone. Matthew 14:23*

Jesus was busy, but He set aside His busyness and made time to pray. The fact that we do not make time to pray reveals that we lack a proper understanding of prayer. There is nothing as essential, as exciting, or as amazing as being able to talk personally to the Lord of the universe!

When we pray, we are cultivating a living, vital relationship with God. As we come to know God better, our knowledge grows from an informative knowledge, to an intellectual knowledge, and finally to an intimate knowledge.

INFORMATIVE KNOWLEDGE OF GOD

There is a universal knowledge of God, the basic knowledge everybody has. We may call this the informative knowledge of God.

At Bible college, I came to have an informative knowledge of the young lady who would later become my wife. I learned some basic facts: her name was Dana, she was the dean's daughter, she was in her 20's, and she had a brother named Matt and a sister named Sarah. This was my informative knowledge of Dana. To some extent, we all have this kind of knowledge of God.

> *The heavens declare the glory of God; and the firmament sheweth his handywork. Day unto day uttereth speech, and night unto night sheweth knowledge. There is no speech nor language, where their voice is not heard. Psalm 19:1-3*

This passage simply means that the glory of God is communicated to people through the skies and the vastness of the universe. This knowledge is given to everyone everywhere and to those of every language and culture. We all share the same sun and the same moon. The stars are out there for all of us to see.

We find this truth again in Romans 1:20: "For the invisible things of him from the creation of the world are clearly seen, being understood by the things that are made, even his eternal power and Godhead; so that they are without excuse." We can gain a knowledge of God as we view His creation – both out in the cosmos and here on earth. Those who see the creation but do not acknowledge the Creator are "without excuse." God has provided all of the evidence necessary for us to come to the proper conclusion.

We do not need to ask ourselves, "How could there be a God?" It would be much more logical to ask, "How could there not be a God?" Everything fits together so perfectly that we should understand there must be a Master Designer. When we conclude there is a God and that He is big enough, powerful enough, and wise enough to create all that we see, we have the informative knowledge of God.

INTELLECTUAL KNOWLEDGE OF GOD

There is another kind of knowledge that we may call the intellectual knowledge of God. This is knowledge about the person of Jesus, but without the experience of His personality. This is knowing the Man but not His manners. It is only an accumulation of facts. Facts and information are important, but there is more to a relationship with God than just a list of facts.

My brother-in-law, Matt, is a big Ronald Reagan fan. He has a large collection of Reagan memorabilia. He knows passages from Reagan's speeches by heart, the chronology of Reagan's presidency, and everything Reagan did before he became President. Did you know that Reagan saved 77 lives as a lifeguard in Dixon, Illinois, and had a brief career as a sports announcer on the radio before he became a movie actor? My brother-in-law knows all these facts, but if you were to ask him if he knew Ronald Reagan, he would declaratively say, "No, I only know about Ronald Reagan. I did not know him."

Similarly, I cannot have an authentic relationship with my wife if I only know about her. Even if I know her favorite color, her favorite flower, her favorite things to do, her favorite places to visit, her birthday, and a lot of other facts, that is not good enough. As her husband, I must get to know her personally and continue to grow in this relationship.

The same can be said about our relationship with God. We can know a lot about what God has done – intellectual knowledge – without ever knowing God for ourselves. To have a relationship with God and be in real communion with Him, we need to know more than just some things about Him; we must actually, know Him personally.

Facts do not equal a relationship. We can know a lot about Jesus and never have a relationship with Him. We cannot build a relationship on intellectual knowledge alone.

THE INTIMATE KNOWLEDGE OF GOD

The intimate knowledge of God is much more important than any informative or intellectual knowledge of God. We can know there is a God and know some things about Him, but above all, God wants us to respond to His love by loving Him in return. This is the genuine relationship God wants us to have with Him.

> *We love him, because he first loved us. 1 John 4:19*

> *But grow in grace, and in the knowledge of our Lord and Saviour Jesus Christ. To him be glory both now and for ever. Amen. 2 Peter 3:18*

From these verses we have a glimpse of the loving relationship that our God wants to have with His people. As the pastor of a church, I do not focus on getting our people to obey the Lord; rather, I try to lead them to love Him. We can obey God without loving Him, but we cannot love God without obeying Him. As we fall in love with the Lord and come to know Him in an intimate way, our obedience will naturally follow.

As we grow in our love for God, we will make time frequently to retreat to a quiet place and have a conversation with Him – to get to know Him. Developing an intimate relationship with God takes time. Often in ministry, pastors do not want to wait for relationships with God to develop; we just want people to perform and behave in a certain way. There are a lot of ministries like this. Legalism is one term used to describe these ministries. Legalism is setting up a bunch of rules and saying, "Follow these rules."

One of the reasons why I think we push so hard in the Christian culture for rules is because we want immediate results. When I preach on prayer, I want everybody to pray, and as a result people pray. But is that the result of people who have a true relationship with God, or are they just following a rule?

Dana and I were talking with a man one day, and my wife asked him if he attended church. He said, "No, I don't, but I pray twice a day. And not some little prayer, but I pray good prayers, like eight-to-nine-minute prayers." That sounds commendable, but do you know what it sounds like? It sounds like legalism. He does this as a routine, and it may have become mechanical. Perhaps he has a stimulating, intimate relationship with his Lord, but I am not sure that he does. Could it be that he prays simply because he knows he should pray? How many of us do the same thing?

Prayer should not be just a ritual; it should be counted a great joy and a privilege. Prayer is a wonderful time where we can communicate with the God of the universe! Prayer should be something we want to do. Our attitude should be, "How could we not pray? Why would we not want to get alone with our Lord who loves us and saved us?"

When we love someone and have a relationship with them, we should love them all the time. We shouldn't only love them on Valentine's Day or Christmas. Prayer, too, is not just something we should do before a meal or as an invocation at a political event; it is something we should do on a constant basis. We cannot always be with the people we love, but the presence of God is with us night and day. He is always available!

Those who have an intimate relationship with God have the keys of prayer to open Heaven's doors. We can and should pray to Him constantly – not just for five minutes, not just at a mid-week prayer meeting, not just on Sunday before church, but all the time.

> *Evening, and morning, and at noon, will I pray, and cry*
> *aloud: and he shall hear my voice. Psalm 55:17*

An old hymn called "I Need Thee Every Hour" expresses this thought well. We must be in constant communion with God all the time. As the Apostle Paul urged us, "Pray without ceasing" (1 Thessalonians 5:17).

In part, prayer is getting alone with God and saying, "Dear God, I need your help!" It is sensitivity and vulnerability. This intimate knowledge of God happens as we experience God working in our lives personally. In many of the Psalms, we see David's fervent expressions of his need for God.

> *O God, thou art my God; early will I seek thee: my soul*
> *thirsteth for thee, my flesh longeth for thee in a dry*
> *and thirsty land, where no water is; To see thy power*
> *and thy glory, so as I have seen thee in the sanctuary.*
> *Psalm 63:1-2*

David was absolutely desperate for the presence of God. As we realize how much we also need God and take the time to get alone with Him, we will find that time escapes us. Right now, you may be asking, "How can I pray for ten minutes?" Just wait until you pray for twenty minutes, and then say, "I can't believe how fast that went by!"

You may think, "I'm too busy to pray." I have found that the busier I am, the more I need to pray. I am so busy that I simply must take the time to be alone with my Lord and Savior. I so desperately need His leading and His help.

A couple of years ago, I had a heart attack. Because of that, I had blood tests done, and the results were not good. High platelets and elevated blood counts – it was a disaster. I was convinced I had cancer. I asked the doctor if I had cancer, and his response was, "I'm not saying." In my thinking, his "not saying" told me a lot, and the blood work seemed to point to cancer. We prayed, and prayed, and prayed, and prayed, and prayed some more. And when we had finished that, we prayed some more.

It was finally time to go to the doctor's office, and get some bloodwork done. They ran the tests, and the results came back. I had resolved that if God allowed cancer in my life, then I would be okay with it and trust Him.

While we were at the office waiting for the doctor, one of the nurses came and asked me, "What have you been doing?"

I said, "We have been praying a lot."

She said, "Because your blood tests are spot on perfect."

I repeated, "I've been praying a lot."

She left, and another nurse came in. She said, "Before the doctor comes in, she wants to know what you have been doing."

I said, "I've been praying a lot. I've been spending a lot of time with my Lord, talking to Him about this."

"Awesome!"

She left, and the doctor came in. She sat down in front of me and said, "What have you been doing?"

I said, "I've been praying a lot."

I am telling you that I experienced the intimate knowledge of God. I experienced the fullness of His power. That is what Job was talking about in Job 42:5: "I have heard of thee by the hearing of the ear: but now mine eye seeth thee." He was saying, "I saw all of the works you have done, Lord. I have experienced the informative and intellectual knowledge of God, but now I really get it." It was not just the testimony of the past saints, or the answered prayers of others, but it was his personal experience. This is the intimate knowledge of God, where you can definitely say, "I spoke, and the Lord heard me. I know He is hearing me, and He wants to help me."

This book is intended to help you be transformed by the renewing of your mind, so you will naturally want to pray. Do you know how this happens? It begins by trusting Christ as your Savior.

What does it mean to trust Christ as your Savior? It simply means that you depend on Christ alone to save you from the penalty of your sin. The Bible says that none are righteous and that all have sinned (Romans 3:10 and 3:23), and that the wages (payment) for that sin is death (Romans 6:23). You must realize that because you are a sinner (someone who has broken God's Law), the payment for your sin is death. The payment isn't joining a church, being water baptized, turning from sin, etc. The payment is death. Somebody must die for your sin.

If you die in your sin, then you will spend an eternity in the Lake of Fire created for the devil and the demons (Matthew 25:41), but God does not want that. He wants you to be saved from this death.

> *[God] Who will have all men to be saved, and to come unto the knowledge of the truth. 1 Timothy 2:4*

In order to save us, God did an absolutely wonderful thing. He sent His Son, Jesus Christ, to die in our place. Jesus Christ came to Earth, lived a perfect life, and then willingly died in our place to pay our sin debt.

> *But God commendeth his love toward us, in that, while we were yet sinners, Christ died for us. Romans 5:8*

Christ died in our place and rose from the dead so we would not have to die for our own sin.

> *For I delivered unto you first of all that which I also received, how that Christ died for our sins according to the scriptures; And that he was buried, and that he rose again the third day according to the scriptures: 1 Corinthians 15:3-4*

By simply believing and trusting what Christ did for us, we are given everlasting life as a free gift.

> *For God so loved the world, that he gave his only begotten Son, that whosoever believeth in him should not perish, but have everlasting life. John 3:16*

> *For the wages of sin is death; but the gift of God is eternal life through Jesus Christ our Lord. Romans 6:23*

Since the payment for sin is death and eternal life is a gift, there is nothing we can do to save ourselves. We cannot pay for sin by being good, and we cannot receive eternal life as a free gift if we work for it. No good work can contribute to your salvation.

> *For by grace are ye saved through faith; and that not of yourselves: it is the gift of God: Not of works, lest any man should boast. Ephesians 2:8-9*

Stop trusting in your church, your baptism, or your works to save you. If you trust in Christ's death and resurrection alone to save you, God promises everlasting life.

> *In hope of eternal life, which God, that cannot lie, promised before the world began; Titus 1:2*

> *These things have I written unto you that believe on the name of the Son of God; that ye may know that ye have eternal life, and that ye may believe on the name of the Son of God. 1 John 5:13*

If you haven't done so yet, believe in what Christ did for you. When you do, you will be guaranteed a home in Heaven, and you will experience God in a brand-new way. You will get your first taste of an intimate relationship with God. As you allow God to work in your life, that relationship will grow more and more intimate, and prayer will become a tremendous joy in your life.

PRAYER POINTS

- The most important aspect of any relationship is communication.

- The fact that we do not make time to pray reveals that we lack a proper understanding of prayer.

- We must know more than just something about God; we must know Him.

- Developing an intimate relationship with God takes time.

- Those who have an intimate relationship with God have the keys of prayer to open Heaven's doors.

2

"When we pray, we can undeniably say, I spoke to the God of the universe..."

The Function of Prayer

Prayer is such a rich and wonderful subject! Although I cannot possibly cover everything about prayer in this book, I hope you will learn much from these words about the tremendous privilege of communicating with God. Beyond learning, though, the goal of this book is for us to experience real prayer. Before we can experience prayer, we must first understand the function of prayer – its purpose. The function of prayer can be described as three things: communication with God, communion with God, and a command from God.

THE COMMUNICATION

My dad lives in Minnesota, and I can communicate with him in a variety of ways. I can send him a text message, and he will respond in a very dad-text-message way – both simple and cryptic. I can call him on the phone, or I could mail a letter to him if technology fails. I do thank God for Apple® and the fact that we can Facetime; I can actually see my dad. While there are all sorts of ways that I can communicate with my dad, there is only one way we can communicate with God: prayer. As children of God, believers must be able to communicate with their heavenly Father. Since prayer is our only means to communicate with Him, we must take time to pray.

But communication is a two-way process. As believers, we deeply need our God to speak to us personally. This is why God gave us the Bible. He speaks to us through His Word and through His Spirit. The Spirit helps us to understand the Scriptures, and He brings those Scriptures into remembrance. Sadly, we neglect to read the Bible even though we can read it at anytime.

The Word of our God should be precious to us. Some time ago, I was given a remarkable story entitled, "How Much Do You Cherish God's Word?" Here is a condensed version:

> William McPherson worked hard and eventually earned the spot of quarry superintendent. Though he had a number of admirable traits, he tended to be a bit impatient. One day his impatience got the best of him, and he grabbed a live stick of dynamite. It exploded, and the accident left him with no hands, little feeling in his face, and no eyesight.
>
> He was now entirely dependent on others to live. On several occasions before, others had tried to share Christ with him; now, due to his accident, he was in a place

to listen. Within a few months he trusted Christ as his savior, but he found he was not satisfied by simply having someone read Scripture to him. He longed for the ability to read it for himself.

Day in and day out he lived in darkness and solitude. One day he learned of a young blind girl who had learned braille and was able to read her Bible with her fingertips. Over time, this young girl lost the feeling in her own hands. She brought the Bible to her lips one day to kiss it goodbye, and to her amazement, she discovered that she could feel the raised letters with her lips!

William had lived in blackness for five years when God sent a blind girl named Anna Johnson to the home where he lived to work with some of the blind patients. William had no hands and no feeling in his face, so the techniques the little girl had adopted would not work. One day, William asked Anna if she could leave with him one of the little cards with which they had been practicing. He kept trying to feel the little raised bumps with different parts of his body when he realized that he had not prayed about it. So he earnestly begged God for help.

The next time he raised the card to his lips, his tongue slipped out and brushed the paper. To his astonishment, he could feel the raised letters with his tongue! William learned how to read braille with his tongue. In the 65

years that followed, through much bleeding and sore-
ness, William read the entire Bible four times with his
tongue.[2]

William's example leaves those of us who can see with no excuse.
He knew that God would speak to him through the Word, and he
wanted to read it for himself. We have the Bible and we know this
is how God communicates to us, and yet for the most part, we do
not really cherish the Scriptures and read them as faithfully as we
ought. This can only be because we do not want strongly enough
to have an intimate relationship with God.

To have a close relationship with God, we must have a deep
desire to communicate with Him – a desire for Him to communicate with us through His Word, and a desire to communicate with
Him through prayer. Unfortunately, many Christians often fail at
both reading and praying.

An online survey conducted by the Barna Research Group in
June 2017 showed that a large majority of Americans claim to
rely on prayer as a means to communicate with God or with their
conception of a "higher power." The study found that prayer is the
most common faith practice among adults, with 79% of the popu-
lation engaging in prayer at least once in the last three months.[3]
Overall, people seem to believe in prayer but do not frequently
practice it.

Surprisingly, even pastors struggle with the matter of prayer. A
2005 Ellison Research survey found that just 16% of pastors are
very satisfied with their personal prayer lives. 47% are somewhat
satisfied, 30% are somewhat dissatisfied, and 7% are very dissatisfied.[4]

So according to this survey, over 1/3 of pastors, the ones who are supposed to be leading others spiritually, are dissatisfied with their personal prayer lives. May I share something with you from my heart? I am very dissatisfied with my own prayer life. I must confess that I am not one who spends hours with the Lord in prayer each day. I do not always pray with faith. No, I would say that I fall within the 7% of the very dissatisfied. My dissatisfaction, however, prompts me to action. I want to do better in this, and I am working on it.

It should be shameful to us that we communicate so little with the God who loves us so much. He wants to speak to us through His Word, and yet we neglect to read it. We can pray anywhere and anytime, but we neglect this as well.

My dad and I were talking about smartphones and videos one day, and I commented, "I am so glad that we don't use old methods, like in the past, to capture video. It used to be really hard, but now anybody can video anything and everything with an iPhone®."

My dad said, "Joe, video your kids, but make sure you are in it. I would give anything to see my dad for 60 seconds." His dad had passed away years before, and now he would give anything to see him just for one minute – not to mention to be able to talk with him. If you were to ask my dad if he would be willing to read a letter from his father in braille with his tongue, I am certain he would say, "Yes, I would do anything as long as I could hear him."

David, the shepherd boy who became king of Israel, desperately longed for the presence of God. Many of his Psalms are actually prayers.

> *O God, thou art my God; early will I seek thee: my soul*
> *thirsteth for thee, my flesh longeth for thee in a dry*
> *and thirsty land, where no water is; To see thy power*
> *and thy glory, so as I have seen thee in the sanctuary.*
> *Psalm 63:1-2*

The heading of this Psalm reads, "A Psalm of David, when he was in the wilderness of Judah." David at this time was on the run, in fear for his life. He knew God was his only hope, so he prayed with the same sense of desperation a dying man in the desert would feel. His communication with God kept him going because he knew God was listening. In other Psalms, David testified of this fact.

> *I have called upon thee, for thou wilt hear me, O God:*
> *incline thine ear unto me, and hear my speech.*
> *Psalm 17:6*
>
> *I cried unto God with my voice, even unto God with my*
> *voice; and he gave ear unto me. Psalm 77:1*

David was certain that the God of the universe heard him, and we can have the same certainty that God hears our prayers. When we pray, we can undeniably say, "I spoke to the God of the universe..."

I love the Jewish people; I honor and appreciate them very much. Yet, when we are at the Western Wall in Israel, it is disheartening to see people put their prayers on paper into the wall. It is sad because they are trying to make sure God receives their prayers by putting them in a place they believe is special to Him. They don't have a relationship with God that assures them that God hears them wherever they are. They don't have a certainty that prayers mean just as much to God at home as they do by the Temple Mount. As Christians, we have a certainty that God hears our prayers anywhere.

The writer of the book of Hebrews relays a blessed invitation: "Let us therefore come boldly unto the throne of grace, that we may obtain mercy, and find grace to help in time of need" (Hebrews 4:16). God has all we need; we simply need to ask. This is communication with God. This is prayer.

THE COMMUNION

Communication is the place to start, but communion runs deeper. One definition of communion is "the sharing or exchanging of intimate thoughts and feelings."[5] As we pray and open our hearts to God, we find a real fellowship and intimacy with Him. In yet another Psalm, David said, "The LORD is nigh unto all them that call upon him, to all that call upon him in truth" (Psalm 145:18). "Nigh" is an old-fashioned word meaning "near." Communion with God is nearness to God, and prayer is part of the way we achieve communion. It is how we draw near to God. As the Bible commands and promises, "Draw nigh to God, and he will draw nigh to you" (James 4:8).

My children and I have a relationship: a father-son relationship. We will always have this relationship, but I want something greater than that. Deeper relationships are the result of deeper communion. I want to be close to my children, and I want them to want to be close to me. In the same way, God wants us to be close to Him. When Jesus wanted to commune with His Father, how did He do it? He prayed.

And in the morning, rising up a great while before day, he went out, and departed into a solitary place, and there prayed. Mark 1:35

And it came to pass in those days, that he went out into a mountain to pray, and continued all night in prayer to God. Luke 6:12

Even Jesus, the Son of God, needed times of communion with His Father. So, He went out and prayed. If we truly want to commune with God, we will need to do the same. We will need to go out, get away – physically if possible, but certainly mentally and spiritually. We will need to put aside our preoccupations and deliberately "draw nigh to God." Dr. R. A. Torrey wrote, "There is no greater joy on earth or in heaven, than communion with God, and prayer in the name of Jesus brings us into communion with Him."[6]

I love communing with my Lord. I have found that spending quality time with Him requires no agenda. We do not need a specific reason to come to Him. We simply need to experience His presence, and He welcomes our communion anytime, anywhere.

Sometimes my sons and I will do something just to be together. There is no plan – only Ben, Josh, and me. There are times that they will be playing with Legos®, and I will come in, get down on the floor, and start stacking blocks. I just want to spend time with my boys.

Although I know that God already knows all about me, I find it exciting to come into communion with Christ and explain, "Lord, this is my feeling right now; this is what is going on in my life." Going to the Lord and knowing that He will help bear my burdens is a wonderful aspect of this communion. I often go to Jesus with thanksgiving, gratefulness, prayer, and supplication, but there are times when I get alone and just tell Him, "Lord, I don't even know what to say. I just want to spend time with You." I simply commune with my Savior.

In March of 2019, I broke a tooth on a cookie. It was a $1,200 cookie or so the dentist's office told me. As I drove away, dismayed by the size of the estimate, I told the Lord, "I don't know how I'm going to pay for this. I don't have the answer; it's a lot of money." I said, "Lord, no agenda, I don't know." A few hours later, I received a call telling me that they were going to fix the tooth for $400 or less. God answered a prayer when I did not even know what to pray for. I was simply communing with the Lord and sharing my burden with Him.

"Take Your Burden to the Lord and Leave It There," wrote the preacher and songwriter Charles A. Tindley. Do you sit down sometimes in your quiet time, close your eyes, and say, "Lord, I love You. I have all sorts of needs, but you know them. I'm not here to ask You anything. I just want to talk with You, Lord, and share with You my struggle and burden"? Beyond communication, do you take the opportunity to commune with your Lord?

The joy of having our prayers answered is never as great as the joy of communing with God. However, when we have communion with God more consistently, our prayers will be answered more consistently.

THE COMMAND

We pray to communicate and commune with God. Did you know we should also pray as a matter of obedience to God? In addition to encouraging us to pray, He actually commands us to pray. The Bible contains many commands when it comes to prayer.

- Matthew 26:41 is a command of Christ to His disciples: "<u>Watch and pray</u>, that ye enter not into temptation: the spirit indeed is willing, but the flesh is weak" (emphasis mine). This command tells us how to avoid temptation. Watch for anything that may bring temptation (be vigilant), and at the same time, pray that you will avoid temptation.

- Roman 12:12 is part of a series of commands: "Rejoicing in hope; patient in tribulation; <u>continuing instant in prayer</u>" (emphasis mine). How long do we wait before we begin to pray to our God? When something is bothering us, when we need communion with our heavenly Father, Paul says to be "instant in prayer," literally constant or ever enduring - similar to 1 Thessalonians 5:17.

- 1 Thessalonians 5:17 puts the command into very simple terms: "<u>Pray without ceasing</u>" (emphasis mine).

- Ephesians 6:18 is one of the commands listed in the context of putting on the armor of God so that we may stand strongly for Him in evil days: "<u>Praying always</u> with all prayer and supplication in the Spirit, and watching thereunto with all perseverance and supplication for all saints" (emphasis mine).

- Luke 18:1 states, "And he spake a parable unto them to this end, that men ought <u>always to pray</u>, and not to faint (emphasis mine)."

These are commands. These are not options; they are obligations. God says to pray always and pray without ceasing. God did not command us to do something that is impossible to do. There must be a way that we can be in a constant state of prayer.

We can be in a constant state of prayer in our subconscious, where we continually think about our heavenly Father and talk with Him. Consider a mother who is constantly thinking about her baby. In the middle of the night when she is sound asleep, she will still hear the baby cry. In her subconscious, she is alert and in tune with that baby. We can and should be continually alert to God - just as the mother who hears her baby cry in the middle of the night.

When I began to pastor in Iowa, my wife and I would drive from the northwest suburbs of Chicago to Davenport, Iowa, and back each weekend. We did that for seven months. We would leave Iowa after a time of fellowship following our Sunday evening service. Since I had to be at work at 5:00 a.m., Dana would usually be driving, with me in a dead sleep. When we would pull into our garage in Chicago, usually around midnight, I would feel that one-inch bump in the pavement, and somewhere in my subconscious, I would know we were home. Similarly, when we are in a constant state of prayer, we are always aware of God, communicating and communing with Him in our subconscious. It will affect everything we do because we are praying all the time.

Not only are we commanded to pray constantly, but we are also commanded to pray for others.

I exhort therefore, that, first of all, supplications, prayers, intercessions, and giving of thanks, be made for all men; For kings, and for all that are in authority;

> *that we may lead a quiet and peaceable life in all*
> *godliness and honesty. 1 Timothy 2:1-2*

Oswald Chambers said, "For whom am I withholding God's blessing by failing to pray for them?"[7] It becomes our fault when others don't get blessed because we're not praying for them.

> *Moreover as for me, God forbid that I should sin*
> *against the LORD in ceasing to pray for you: but I will*
> *teach you the good and the right way: 1 Samuel 12:23*

Because God commands us to pray, we need to understand, as Samuel did, that prayerlessness is a sin. Dr. John R. Rice wrote a wonderful book called Prayer: Asking and Receiving, and in it, he confessed:

> "My greatest sin, and yours, is prayerlessness. My fail-
> ures are all prayer-failures. The lack of souls saved in
> my ministry is primarily because of lack of prayer, not
> because of lack of preaching. The withering away of joy
> in my heart, sometimes is the fruit of prayerlessness.
> My indecision, my lack of wisdom, my lack of guidance
> come directly out of my prayerlessness. All the times I
> have fallen into sin, have failed in my duties, have been
> bereft of power, or disconsolate for lack of comfort, I
> can charge to the sin of prayerlessness."[8]

Think about the statement, "My failures are all prayer-failures." Every time we fail, it is because we fail in prayer! We must pray more – in both communication and communion – simply out of obedience. Not to pray and not to spend intimate time with our Lord is a sin. Many of us abide in the sin of prayerlessness. We are so quick to run to other sources for answers to our questions and our needs, but we fail to go directly to the throne of grace.

How desperate are you to speak to God? How desperate are you to know God? Are you as desperate to hear from God as William McPherson was – willing to read the Bible with his tongue? That was a man who really wanted to know and hear from God. God really wants to hear from you too, so make sure you make time to pray.

PRAYER POINTS

- The function of prayer can be described as three things: communication with God, communion with God, and a command from God.

- To have a close relationship with God, we must have a deep desire to communicate with Him – a desire for Him to communicate with us through His Word, and a desire to communicate with Him through prayer.

- As we pray and open our hearts to God, we find a real fellowship and intimacy (communion) with Him.

- God says to pray always and pray without ceasing. God did not command us to do something that is impossible to do.

- Many of us abide in the sin of prayerlessness. We are so quick to run to other sources for answers to our questions and our needs, but we fail to go directly to the throne of grace.

3

"Time spent in prayer
is not wasted, but time
invested at big interest."

R. A. Torrey

The Foundation of Prayer

As a former contractor, I can tell you that a good foundation is important to the integrity of a building. A poor foundation will eventually cause the whole structure to fail.

An investor once employed me to buy houses for him with the intention of rehabbing them, renting them out, and eventually selling them. A house would usually look good on paper, but I needed to see it for myself. As the realtor and I approached the house, I would look it over quickly and sometimes just tell him to keep driving; I had seen everything I needed to see. From a distance, I would look for bowed gutters and an uneven roof line. If I did go inside, I would look for cracked drywall in certain places. These were all strong indications of problems with the foundation. We knew that a faulty foundation would sooner or later affect the entire house, and we would not consider buying it unless the price reflected the cost of repairing the foundation.

The foundation makes all the difference in buildings and even in life. As Jesus concluded His "Sermon on the Mount," He said this:

> *Therefore whosoever heareth these sayings of mine, and doeth them, I will liken him unto a wise man, which built his house upon a rock: And the rain descended, and the floods came, and the winds blew, and beat upon that house; and it fell not: for it was founded upon a rock. And every one that heareth these sayings of mine, and doeth them not, shall be likened unto a foolish man, which built his house upon the sand: And the rain descended, and the floods came, and the winds blew, and beat upon that house; and it fell: and great was the fall of it. Matthew 7:24-27*

Just as the foundation of a building and the foundation of life are vital, the foundation of our prayers is also vital. Before we even start to pray, we must remember who we are and to whom we are praying; these are foundational matters.

To pray effectively, we must first know who God is. Unfortunately, in today's culture we have a very twisted view of God. I have talked with Christians and non-Christians alike who see God as a tyrant: heavy-handed, mean-spirited, and tight-fisted. Let me assure you that while God does deal firmly with sin, He is so much more than just a judge. If you tend to think of God negatively, I pray this chapter will change your impression of Him. When your view of God changes, your prayer life will also change.

THE FAITHFULNESS OF THE SAVIOR

God's love, God's goodness, and God's mercy are foundational to His character and to our understanding of who He is. Without a strong belief in these characteristics, why would we even pray? Why would we pray to a God who does not love us, and who is not good? Why would we pray for mercy to a God who is not merciful? But we can rejoice and pray because we know we have a faithful Savior, worthy of all our trust.

LIMITLESS LOVE

If we want to know the faithfulness of the Savior, we must first understand that His love for us is limitless. There are no bounds, no restrictions. "God is love," as the Apostle John told us (1 John 4:8). As God Himself is infinite, so is the love of God.

We see that God's limitless love is an eternal love. God's love always has been and always will be.

> *The LORD hath appeared of old unto me, saying, Yea, I have loved thee with an everlasting love: therefore with lovingkindness have I drawn thee. Jeremiah 31:3*

Everlasting love – think on that for a moment. It is a love that lasts forever and never ends! John expressed this kind of love when he wrote, "Having loved his own which were in the world, *he loved them unto the end*" (John 13:1, emphasis mine). If you understand the eternal love of God, it will change our view of prayer. We can pray in full confidence that there is nothing we can do to change or to forfeit that love. Romans 8:35-39 says that nothing can separate us from the love of God.

Did you know that God loves us the same today as He did yesterday and as He will tomorrow? Hebrews 13:8 says, "Jesus Christ the same yesterday, and to day, and for ever." His love is unchanging and eternal. Although my life has many ups and downs, there is one thing I can always count on: He is a faithful Savior, and He never stops loving me. Knowing this, I can always feel welcome when I come to Him in prayer.

God's limitless love is also a great love. It is eternal, not limited by time, and great, not limited by capacity.

> *But God, who is rich in mercy, for his great love wherewith he loved us, Even when we were dead in sins, hath quickened us together with Christ, (by grace ye are saved;) Ephesians 2:4-5*

Many of us have dreamed of being rich, of having an unlimited source of money - well our God is rich in mercy.

The songwriter Charles H. Gabriel expressed God's great love and mercy when he wrote:

> I stand amazed in the presence,
> Of Jesus the Nazarene,
> And wonder how He could love me,
> A sinner, condemned, unclean.

It takes a great love to bridge the great chasm our sin created between ourselves and a holy God. Our faithful Savior has that great kind of love. God's limitless love is also a sacrificial love, not limited by consideration of self. In the second verse of "I Stand Amazed," Gabriel expressed this selfless love:

> For me it was in the garden,
> He prayed, "Not my will, but thine,"
> He had no tears for his own griefs,
> But sweat drops of blood for mine.[9]

Lewis Sperry Chafer said, "There is no selfishness in divine love. God has never sought benefits for Himself. He receives nothing; He bestows everything."[10]

> *Hereby perceive we the love of God, because he laid down his life for us: 1 John 3:16*

This selfless, great love ought to encourage us to pray! We can know that God loves us because He died for us. If we ever needed evidence of God's limitless love, here it is: Christ died for our sins on the cross – freely laying down His life for us.

When I spend time with my faithful Savior in prayer, I think about how He loves me with an eternal, great, and sacrificial love. His love truly is limitless!

GRAND GOODNESS

As we consider the foundation of prayer, as we come to understand more about the God to whom we are praying, we see that God's love is limitless, and also that His goodness is grand. To call the Lord "good" seems almost like an understatement, but the Bible refers to God as being good.

> *O taste and see that the LORD is good: blessed is the man that trusteth in him. Psalm 34:8*

> *Enter into his gates with thanksgiving, and into his courts with praise: be thankful unto him, and bless his name. For the LORD is good; his mercy is everlasting;*

> *and his truth endureth to all generations.*
> *Psalm 100:4-5*

The Lord is good. The word "good" can bring to our minds many associations. We think of good food as being pleasant to the taste. We think of good friends as being congenial company. We think of a good car as being reliable. Our God is pleasant, congenial, reliable, and so much more!

> *Oh that men would praise the LORD for his goodness,*
> *and for his wonderful works to the children of men!*
> *Psalm 107:31*

Very simply and yet in the richest sense of the word, God is good. Just His goodness alone should encourage us to pray and praise Him for who He is.

I hear people say all the time that they struggle with praying. I ask them what their view of God is, and their response answers a lot of questions. They might say, "Oh yes, God is love. The Bible says that, and I'm thankful for it. God loves the world, but maybe He isn't personally interested in me." It is sad to hear Christians talk like that because this is such a twisted, distorted view of our faithful Savior. They don't see God's goodness. Nothing can separate us from the limitless, eternal love of a good God!

MEASURELESS MERCY

As God's love is limitless and His goodness is grand, so His mercy is measureless. We have already spoken of God's mercy, as Ephesians 2:4 speaks of "God, who is rich in mercy." It is overflowing and constant. He has all the mercy we will ever need.

Many Bible verses refer to the mercy of God, and as you look at these you will notice that the concepts of His love, His goodness, and His mercy are closely related.

The LORD is merciful and gracious, slow to anger, and plenteous in mercy. Psalm 103:8

But the mercy of the LORD is from everlasting to everlasting upon them that fear him, and his righteousness unto children's children; Psalm 103:17

To express the truth of God's mercy being without measure, the Psalmist who wrote Psalm 136 ended all 26 verses in that Psalm with the phrase, "For his mercy endureth forever." Truly God's mercy is measureless!

What exactly is mercy? It is God choosing not to give us the punishment we actually deserve. Because of God's mercy, "he will not forsake thee, neither destroy thee" (Deuteronomy 4:31). Because of God's mercy, He is "slow to anger" (Psalm 103:8). We deserve nothing except God's immediate and final wrath on our sin, and yet He extends mercy. Christ suffered the wrath of God in our place, and so God has mercy on us.

People tend to think that God is quick to anger and lacks mercy, yet the Bible constantly insists the opposite. Psalm 103:13-14 states, "Like as a father pitieth his children, so the LORD pitieth them that fear him. For he knoweth our frame; he remembereth that we are dust."

Recently, I went out to eat for breakfast. The waitress brought me a glass of orange juice, and it was full to the brim. I almost had to put my lips down and drink it while it was on the table. That is what we call full. Nothing was lacking: nothing fell short. In the same way, God is full of mercy, full to the brim.

> *But thou, O Lord, art a God full of compassion, and gracious, longsuffering, and plenteous in mercy and truth. Psalm 86:15*

> *The LORD is gracious, and full of compassion; slow to anger, and of great mercy. Psalm 145:8*

Grace, compassion, mercy – full, plenteous, and great. As we read His Word and become more and more familiar with the faithfulness of our Savior, we see that our God is not out to get us. He is not looking down on us with a constant frown, waiting for us to mess up so He can punish us. He delights in showing us His limitless love, His grand goodness, and His measureless mercy.

If God wasn't faithful, loving, good, or merciful, it would be a complete waste of time to pray. But as R. A. Torrey said, "Time spent in prayer is not wasted, but time invested at big interest."[11] Praise God that when we pray, we are investing; we're not wasting! We are talking to a God who loves us so much, who is infinitely merciful, and who is more than capable of dealing with our problems. The better we know God, the more we will want to pray.

THE FAILURES OF THE SINNER

If it were not for the failures of the sinner, there would be no need for the faithfulness of the Savior. We must have a right view of ourselves, for this is just as foundational to prayer as having a right view of our Savior. People say there is a self-esteem problem in America, and yes, there is. Yet, the problem is not low self-esteem; rather, it is just the opposite. People think of themselves more highly than they ought to think. We call that pride.

When the prophet Isaiah saw the Lord as He really was, he was able to see himself as he really was. As he looked at himself, he did not like what he saw.

> *Then said I, Woe is me! for I am undone; because I am a man of unclean lips, and I dwell in the midst of a people of unclean lips: for mine eyes have seen the King, the LORD of hosts. Isaiah 6:5*

Whatever self-esteem Isaiah may have had was gone in a flash. As we also look at ourselves and compare ourselves to a holy God, we see our unholiness and our sin. Our sin demands a penalty that only Jesus could pay. And out of His limitless love, His grand goodness, and His measureless mercy, our faithful Savior did just that.

As I mentioned earlier, Dr. John R. Rice said, "My failures are all prayer-failures."[12] May I broaden that a little bit? I would say that all of my failures are related to my sin. My failures are always sin failures, and prayerlessness is one symptom of the basic problem. We will look at several of our failures in this chapter, and hopefully, we will see ourselves in light of a holy God.

SIN OF INDEPENDENCE

We normally think of independence as a good thing. We remember 1776 as the year America declared independence. Financial independence is desirous for everyone. The problem is that many of us also want to live independently from God.

Why is this? People want to keep a distance from God because they do not want God to invade all of their lives. They want to be their own authority and live their own way. They fail to realize that

God gives them every breath and every heartbeat. If not for Him, they would not live another second.

In John 15, Jesus used the example of a grapevine and its branches to illustrate the dependence of God's people on Him: "Without me ye can do nothing" (John 15:5). A branch separated from the vine soon becomes nothing but a dead stick.

In another context, Jesus said that "with God all things are possible" (Matthew 19:26). We can do nothing without God, but with Him we can do everything. That alone is reason enough to pray to Him. We cannot be independent from God; we need Him morning, noon, and night.

> *Evening, and morning, and at noon, will I pray, and cry aloud: and he shall hear my voice. Psalm 55:17*

R. A. Torrey said, "Prayer often avails where everything else fails."[13] Why is that? Because with God we can do everything, and without Him, we can do nothing. No wonder everything else seems to fail until we recognize that we are not independent from God and bring God our burdens in prayer! No wonder prayer avails at that moment!

When I pray, I often visualize myself on my knees before Christ at the cross. When I pray, I view who I am in light of who God is. He is not my equal. He goes far beyond that. When I pray, I relinquish my independence from God, and I depend on Him. Proper prayer is the very opposite of independence.

SIN OF IDOLATRY

Idolatry? "I don't pray to statues," you might say. Indeed, the commandment, "Thou shalt have no other gods before me"

(Exodus 20:3), speaks directly of graven images. But the larger principle is the injunction against putting anything or anybody in the place of the true and living God.

Honestly, most of the time we idolize ourselves. The sin of idolatry goes hand in hand with the sin of independence. We want to get away from God, and we justify it by elevating ourselves above God. We become our own idols. The book of Judges tells the story of a long and sad period in the history of Israel, brought about because "every man did that which was right in his own eyes" (Judges 17:6, 21:25). The Bible also says in Proverbs 14:12, "There is a way which seemeth right unto a man, but the end thereof are the ways of death." When people put themselves above God, it never ever turns out well.

Prayer is the opposite of idolatry. It is putting God in His proper place. He is everything; we are nothing. He is the authority; our part is to obey. He is the provider; we are the needy ones.

SIN OF IMMORALITY

Here is the downward spiral: independence and idolatry always lead to immorality. As people reject God and His ways, sin is the invariable result. "Whosoever committeth sin transgresseth also the law: for sin is the transgression of the law" (1 John 3:4). A transgression is a violation of God's law.

The Apostle John tells us that "God is light, and in him is no darkness at all" (1 John 1:5). When we reject the light, we will find nothing but darkness. If God has absolutely no darkness in Him, and we are independent from Him, where will we be? In darkness. When we're in darkness, we don't pray as we ought to pray, we don't love God as we ought to love Him, and we are becoming independent from God.

Those who reject the morals of God have nothing left but immorality. Romans chapter 1 graphically highlights the trend of those who reject God:

> *Because that, when they knew God, they glorified him not as God, neither were thankful; but became vain in their imaginations, and their foolish heart was darkened. Professing themselves to be wise, they became fools, And changed the glory of the uncorruptible God into an image made like to corruptible man, and to birds, and fourfooted beasts, and creeping things. Wherefore God also gave them up to uncleanness. . .*
> *Romans 1:21-24*

In this passage we see the failures of the sinner, progressing from independence to idolatry to immorality. In such a state, who would dare to pray to a holy God? Only those who understand the faithfulness of the Savior in His limitless love, His grand goodness, and His measureless mercy! This is the foundation of prayer: seeing God for who He is and ourselves for who we are.

Thank God for a faithful Savior. You have failures as a sinner, and your failures keep you from having a right relationship with God. Yet, His faithfulness is what allows you to have a wonderful relationship with your heavenly Father. Remember these foundational truths when you are praying.

PRAYER POINTS

- A poor foundation will eventually cause the whole structure to fail.

- Before we even start to pray, we must remember who we are and to whom we are praying; these are foundational matters.

- When your view of God changes, your prayer life will change.

- If it were not for the failures of the sinner, there would be no need for the faithfulness of the Savior.

- Proper prayer is the very opposite of independence, it is total dependence on God.

4

"The authority of the
Word of God is vital in
our prayer life."

The Faith of Prayer

Faith is one of the most misunderstood concepts of prayer, but we need to understand its role if we want to pray the way God wants us to pray. "I believe God," the Apostle Paul proclaimed in Acts 27:25. This is faith in a nutshell. The more we believe God, the more eager and effective our prayers will be to God.

THE ESSENTIALISM OF FAITH

Traditionally, man's basic needs have been listed as food, shelter, and clothing. For His people, God would add one more item to the list: faith. Faith is not just important; it is essential to the Christian life and to prayer.

FAITH IS ESSENTIAL FOR PLEASING GOD

"The difficult we do immediately. The impossible takes a little longer" was a motto used by the U.S. armed forces during World War II. But when God says something is impossible, it truly is impossible. Here is something that God says is impossible:

> But without faith it is impossible to please him: for he
> that cometh to God must believe that he is, and that he
> is a rewarder of them that diligently seek him.
> Hebrews 11:6

We are unable to please God without faith, without belief. What are we to believe? The same verse answers that question.

First, we must believe in God's existence, "believe that he is." When we come to God, we must believe we are coming to the true and living God. In the last chapter, we discussed seeing God as He is. We must come to God with the realization of who He is: holy and righteous, with limitless love, grand goodness, and measureless mercy.

Second, we must believe that we will not come to Him in vain and leave empty-handed, "that he is a rewarder of them that diligently seek him." As we come to God in faith, diligently seeking Him, we know that we will be rewarded. We may not get what we want, but we will get what we need. This is faith, without which it is impossible to please God.

There was no permanent baptistry in our previous church building. When we wanted to baptize someone, we had to bring in a baptistry, fill it, and heat up the water. A church member stored the baptistry in his barn. When we needed to use it and the fellow said that he could bring it to church, I never wondered if he had the ability to bring it. I did not ask if his truck was capable of moving it. I did not question whether he would actually come through on his promise. I was confident in him because I knew him well enough to know he would bring the baptistry when I needed it, and he appreciated my confidence in him.

Why do we so often put more faith in people than we put in God? Believe God! Trusting God to deliver on His promises pleases Him. Faith is essential for pleasing God.

FAITH IS ESSENTIAL FOR OBEYING GOD

> *And Jesus answering saith unto them, Have faith in God. Mark 11:22*

Jesus says we are to have faith in God. This is a command. It is not an option but an obligation. When we do not have faith in God, we are disobeying Him, and that is sin. Most people would excuse a lack of faith, but God does not.

Romans 14:23 states, "For whatsoever is not of faith is sin." If we do not have faith, it is sin, but also, if we do not act in faith, it is sin. 1 Corinthians 10:31 says, "Whether therefore ye eat, or drink, or whatsoever ye do, do all to the glory of God." Faith is something we are to have, but it is also something we are to live. We usually find faith and action coupled together in Scripture. Read through Hebrews chapter 11. Time after time, this chapter mentions what various people did because of what they believed. Their faith prompted them to action. They trusted what God had said and how he directed, and then they acted in faith to carry out God's will. Faith is essential for obeying God.

THE EDUCATION OF FAITH

Yes, faith is essential to teach us. As we watch our faith grow, we can look back and see how much we've learned during that time. The disciples are a great example of this truth.

THE DISCIPLES LACKED FAITH

> *And he said unto them, Why are ye so fearful? how is it that ye have no faith? Mark 4:40*

Jesus asked these very pointed questions of His disciples, just after He had stilled a storm on the Sea of Galilee.

The first time I hosted a trip to Israel, a small group of people from our church were just about to get onto a boat on the Sea of Galilee. Our guide, David, looked at the sky and said, "We might want to wait out the storm." It didn't look all that menacing to us, but we followed his advice, went over to a nearby building, and stood outside under a shelter. The storm came up quickly, and a bolt of lightning, like the finger of God, struck right in front of us. The wind was howling, the rain was coming down sideways, and then suddenly the storm just stopped. The sun came out, and we were able to sail. When I now read the accounts of these storms whipping up on the Sea of Galilee, I have first-hand experience of how quickly these storms appear and what the disciples may have encountered.

We must remember that the disciples were already out on the sea when the storm came up. Although several of them were experienced fishermen and had no doubt been in storms before, this one was especially bad, and they knew their lives were in danger. They looked at Jesus and cried out in desperation, "Carest thou not that we perish?" (Mark 4:38). Of course Jesus cared, so He calmed the storm. Then, with the crisis past, He asked them why they had so much fear and no faith.

It is interesting to me that He had to ask the question, "How is that ye have no faith?" By this time in Jesus' ministry, He had already proven Himself time and time again:

Mark 1:25 – He healed the one with the unclean spirit.
Mark 1:41 – He cleansed the leper.
Mark 2:11 – He healed the paralytic.
Mark 3:5 – He healed the man with the withered hand.

The disciples had seen what Jesus could do, so why were they so frightened now and wondering if He cared? Why did they not have the faith and confidence they should have had? It is because, ultimately, they were just like us. We have seen God's faithfulness over and over again in our lives, but still there are times we question whether God can perform His promises. We should take this question to heart: "How is that ye have no faith?"

Quite evidently, the faith of the disciples grew. In the book of Acts, after Christ had ascended to Heaven, we find them performing mighty works and speaking boldly in the name of the Lord.

> *But Peter, standing up with the eleven, lifted up his voice, and said unto them, Ye men of Judaea, and all ye that dwell at Jerusalem, be this known unto you, and hearken to my words: Acts 2:14*

So began a sermon that culminated in three thousand people coming to salvation in Christ (Acts 2:41). The passage continues,

"And they continued stedfastly in the apostles' doctrine and fellowship, and in breaking of bread, and in prayers. And fear came upon every soul: and many wonders and signs were done by the apostles" (Acts 2:42-43). These same men who at one time had much fear and no faith were now fearless and faithful. Oh, how much they changed because they learned to have faith in God!

THE DISCIPLES DIDN'T KNOW HOW TO PRAY

And it came to pass, that, as he was praying in a certain place, when he ceased, one of his disciples said unto him, Lord, teach us to pray, as John also taught his disciples. Luke 11:1

Christ's disciples did not start out as awesome prayer warriors. After witnessing the miracles of Mark 1, 2, and 3, the disciples should have had enough faith to be great prayer warriors by the occasion of the storm on the sea in chapter 4. Yet, in Luke 11, we find the disciples asking Jesus to teach them how to pray, as though they knew nothing about it. To their credit, though, they wanted to learn. They wanted to grow!

D.L. Moody said, "We are not told that Jesus ever taught his disciples how to preach, but he taught them how to pray. He wanted them to have power with God; then he knew they would have power with man."[14] Preaching is our communication to man, but prayer is our communication to God. This is why knowing how to pray is much more important than knowing how to preach. Like the disciples, God wants us to learn how to pray. As we draw nigh to God and He draws nigh to us (James 4:8), He will teach us everything we need to know for His service. That is what we learn, the education that comes through faith.

THE EXERCISE OF FAITH

If we are to exercise our faith, we must first have faith. Faith comes through knowing God's Word.

> *So then faith cometh by hearing, and hearing by the word of God. Romans 10:17*

Faith comes from hearing God's Word. Praying in faith is impossible without knowing God's Word. This point is wonderfully explained by R. A. Torrey:

> If we are to have real faith, we must study the Word of God and find out what is promised, then simply believe the promises of God. Faith must have a warrant. Trying to believe something that you want to believe is not faith. . . . If I am to have faith when I pray, I must find some promise in the Word of God on which to rest my faith . . . but in no case does real faith come by simply determining that you are going to get something you want to get."[15]

Faith is finding something in the Word of God and saying, "I can rest my faith on that. What God said in His Word is true, so I am confident of this outcome because that's what God said." Therefore, the authority of the Word of God is vital in our prayer life.

There are a lot of people who do not believe in miracles or the Bible. There are even some Christian people who try to tear apart the Word of God and find all of its flaws. However, the Bible will withstand the test of time.

If we can't trust the Bible to be true, we can't trust the promises of God. If we can't trust the promises of God, what are we resting our faith on? We must base our faith on something, or else we will have flawed promises and have no way to pray in faith. If the Bible is rejected, our faith will not increase, and our prayers will not be answered. We must rest our faith upon something that is reliable, or we will never be able to pray with faith.

Here is a great hymn called, "My Faith Has Found a Resting Place":

> My faith has found a resting place,
> Not in device nor creed;
> I trust the Ever-living One,
> His wounds for me shall plead.
>
> I need no other argument,
> I need no other plea;
> It is enough that Jesus died,
> And that He died for me.
>
> My heart is leaning on the Word,
> The written Word of God,
> Salvation by my Savior's name,
> Salvation through His blood.[16]

If we don't lean on the Word of God, if we don't know for certain that it is true, then we cannot rest our faith on the God of the Bible. If we can't rest our faith on Him, how could we pray to Him in faith?

If we want to improve our prayer life, we must increase our faith. Even Jesus' disciples asked Him to increase their faith.

And the apostles said unto the Lord, Increase our faith.
Luke 17:5

We need to increase our faith when we pray. Often when I pray, I pray so faithlessly – doubting that what I pray will happen. Because of this, I find myself often praying, "Lord, please increase my faith; I want to have better faith than this. I want to have the kind of faith that I know for certain things will come true." But how do we increase our faith?

In order to grow, our faith must be exercised – that is, put to use. Just as unused muscles will deteriorate, unused faith cannot grow in strength and will actually become weaker.

When you stop to think about it, you realize that all types of exercise involve some kind of resistance and the effort to overcome that resistance. Lifting weights or doing pushups is basically a straining against the force of gravity, and as the various muscles push against this resistance – if done correctly, of course – they grow in strength. Conversely, what happens if a person chooses or is forced to spend long periods of time doing nothing physical? The body goes downhill and strength is lost. If you have ever had your arm or leg in a cast, you understand what happens to muscles that are not used.

It is the same with the mind. Older people will often do crossword puzzles or Sudoku in an effort to keep their minds sharp.

The same principle is true with faith. You may have only a little faith. As you exercise the little faith you have, believing God for little things, you will see Him work and demonstrate His faithfulness. You will be encouraged to believe God for bigger things, and as a consequence your faith will grow. Those who know God best tend to have the most faith.

> *If ye have faith as a grain of mustard seed, ye shall say unto this mountain, Remove hence to yonder place; and it shall remove; and nothing shall be impossible unto you. Matthew 17:20*

Jesus was saying that even a little faith (a mustard seed is very tiny), properly placed and in the will of God, can accomplish mighty things. But notice, the faith had to be exercised. If you are not willing to talk to the mountain, that mountain will stay right where it is.

On the matter of exercising faith, I once gave an object lesson in my church. I called up five volunteers to the front of the auditorium. I told them that I represented God for the illustration, and I declared that I wanted to give each of them a king-sized Reese's® Peanut Butter Cup. I declared it was good for them, and that it was my will for their lives. As I said that, I held up three king-sized Reese's® and told the people, "All you have to do to receive one is ask me for it."

The first three people in line did exactly as I bid them, and I gave them the candy bars. When the fourth person came up, she timidly asked, "Could I please have one?" She asked skeptically, even though I had said that I would give her one, and even though everyone before her had asked and received. The reason she was skeptical was because I had no more candy in my hands. Because she could not see the provision, she asked with little faith.

I reached under the pulpit and pulled out another peanut butter cup. Because she had asked for something that I wanted her to have, I willingly gave it to her. Even though her faith was small, she asked, and I kept my word. Then we came to the fifth person. He confidently asked if he could have one, and he received it.

Neither of the last two people had much faith that I would be able to give them a candy bar, but when I gave the lady one when she asked, that increased the man's faith that I would do the same for him if he asked. The difference for the man was not in my ability to give away candy (I had a whole box), but rather, the difference was that his faith increased when he saw what I had given to others.

The people had faith that I was real and that I would reward them. And yet, the faith would have been useless had they not asked, and then reached out and taken what I offered them. As they exercised their faith, their confidence grew.

Don't we have every reason to put our full confidence in God? I say it again: the more we believe God, the more eager and effective our prayers will be. Keeping the illustration in mind, here are three ways to increase your faith:

GET TO KNOW GOD'S WORD BETTER

Faith must have a basis. Through God's Word we know His commandments and His promises. Through His Word, we see His faithfulness. Dr. John R. Rice wrote, "Faith is really depending on God's faithfulness to do what He agrees to do."[17] It comes back to the essence of faith: believing God.

If either of the last two people in my illustration had seen the box of chocolates under the pulpit, they would have never doubted my ability and willingness to give them the candy. They would have had great faith that I would give it to them when they asked.

In the same way, if we want great faith, we must get to know God through His Word. "So then faith cometh by hearing, and hearing by the word of God" (Romans 10:17). We cannot trust in someone we do not know. Faith is developed through learning and understanding the Scriptures. This is why we must read, memorize, and meditate on the Bible.

We must know God's Word to know what He has promised! When we ask God for things He has promised to give us, we can be assured that we will get them. The first three people in my illustration knew they were getting chocolate because they saw it in my hand, and I had promised it to them. The King of Kings and Lord of Lords cannot lie. If He has promised, then He must and will deliver. When I pray, I can actually go to the throne of God and I can say, "Lord, You said this, and I am taking this to the bank. I am going to cash this check because You promised." However, to do that, we have to know what He has promised in His Word.

REMEMBER WHAT HE HAS DONE

When we forget what He has done in the past, we will deny what He said He will do in the future. We must remember those things. If the following week I had called up the same five people and used the same illustration, the lady's faith in my ability to give her a peanut butter cup would have grown considerably because she could say, "He did it before, why wouldn't he do it again?"

Never forget the things God has done. One way you can remember what He has done is by writing things down. Keep prayer journals and write down God's answers to your prayers. Never forget what God has done because that is an example of what He will do in the future. Since He said that He is going to provide, and you remember how He has provided for you in the past, you can smile with joy and say, "Lord, you've always taken care of me before - I know you will take care of me now. I have everything to look forward to."

GET OUT OF HIS WAY

George Mueller said that before one can pray, one's heart must have "no will of its own in regard to a given matter."[18] Sometimes we try to limit God, and we pray, "Lord, here's what You need to do, and here's how You need to do it." Here is a better way to pray: "I don't know what provision looks like, God. All I know is that You said You would provide for me, and however You decide to do it, I'll be fine with it."

God does not always work the way we may want or expect, but He does always fulfill His promises. We must look to Him and pray in faith on any given matter, believing that He always knows what is best and that He always does what is right. If God says He is going to deliver on a promise, He will deliver. We need to trust Him for the "how" and the "when." We need to get out of His way and let Him do His work – in His own way and in His own time.

To put it very simply: When you pray, believe God! Faith is an essential component of prayer and connecting with God.

PRAYER POINTS

- We cannot please God with faithless prayers.
- Our faith should be growing.
- We need to exercise our faith.
- Three ways to increase your faith include:

  Get to know God's Word better.
  Remember what He has done for you in the past.
  Get out of His way and let Him do His work.

5

"Getting alone with God often requires getting away from others."

Gary Miller

The Focus of Prayer

Focusing can be very difficult. There are many people, including myself, who struggle with paying attention. You are probably familiar with Attention Deficit Disorder (ADD). Perhaps I have a touch of ADD, or perhaps my mind just naturally runs a million miles a second. In any case, if you have known me for very long you would probably say, "Joe never stops thinking about something." That is very close to the truth. As a matter of fact, especially when I am working, I get distracted very easily. I will be in the middle of something, and before I know it, I will find myself pacing and thinking of new ideas and things we can do. I really have to fight to focus on the task at hand.

I do not want to minimize ADD. I understand that many people struggle with it. However, I also believe that many think they have an attention disorder, when in reality they only lack discipline. Discipline is needed for focus, so when someone lacks discipline, they lack focus.

When we pray, we must discipline ourselves to focus our attention on prayer – and more importantly, on the One to whom we are praying. Since prayer is communicating with God, we want to have our conversation with Him dialed in. We want to make sure we are focusing.

THE PLACE OF FOCUSED PRAYER

The Gospels show us that Jesus prayed on many different occasions. Let us look at a few specific places where Jesus prayed and learn from them.

THE WILDERNESS PRAYER

> *But so much the more went there a fame abroad of him: and great multitudes came together to hear, and to be healed by him of their infirmities. And he withdrew himself into the wilderness, and prayed. Luke 5:15-16*

Here we find a great example of Jesus' response as He got busier and busier in the ministry. As He began to preach, heal, and do wonderful miracles, He became well-known in Galilee. As a result, the needs of people and the pressures of life bombarded Him. What did He do when He came under so much pressure? He did not plunge in and work harder, as so many people do today. Instead, He "withdrew himself into the wilderness, and prayed." Sometimes we need to withdraw ourselves from the pressures of life and spend focused time with our Lord. How wonderful it is just to get away and pray!

THE MOUNTAIN PRAYER

And it came to pass in those days, that he went out into a mountain to pray, and continued all night in prayer to God. Luke 6:12

Christ's example should become a pattern in our own lives. Deliberately, we need to take time to remove ourselves from the busyness of the world. The world is not going to slow down; we have to slow down, on purpose, on a regular basis. We need our times of refuge, so we need to step away, rise above the pressures of this life, and spend focused time alone with God.

R. A. Torrey wrote, "Nights of prayer to God are followed by days of power with men."[19] Martin Luther has been quoted as saying, "Work, work, from morning until late at night. In fact, I have so much to do that I shall have to spend the first three hours in prayer!"[20]

In our communication with God, we must guard against interruptions. How irritated are we when we are in the middle of talking to someone, and then someone else comes along and takes over the conversation? Does God appreciate it when we allow interruptions to take us away from prayer? Of course not! If we want to focus on prayer, we must not allow interruptions during our conversations with God.

As we communicate with God, we must have a time and place where we can get away from external pressure. We can talk to God in a variety of places, such as while we are driving or while we are in a check-out line. However, just praying anywhere is not the same as getting alone with God and away from distractions.

Focused prayer begins with choosing a location away from distractions. We find this example set by our Lord: a pattern of getting away into the wilderness or mountain and being alone for a time. Location makes a real difference when it comes to focused communication.

THE CLOSET PRAYER

I try very hard to have my time alone with the Lord, but often it is interrupted by all sorts of other activities and random thoughts. Jesus gave a strong command that helps me and will help others who have the same problem:

> *And when thou prayest, thou shalt not be as the hypocrites are: for they love to pray standing in the synagogues and in the corners of the streets, that they may be seen of men. Verily I say unto you, They have their reward. But thou, when thou prayest, enter into thy closet, and when thou hast shut thy door, pray to thy Father which is in secret; and thy Father which seeth in secret shall reward thee openly.*
> *Matthew 6:5-6*

The hypocrites got what they were really hoping for. People looked at them and said, "Wow, good prayer!" And when we pray with the purpose of impressing people, we will get nothing out of it but their admiration. Even that is not guaranteed, but certainly we will get nothing from God. That is why Jesus says in verse 6, "But thou, when thou prayest, enter into thy closet, and when thou hast shut thy door, pray to thy Father which is in secret; and thy Father which seeth in secret shall reward thee openly." When we pray, we need to get alone with God so we will not be tempted to seek praise from men for our pretty prayers. Alone and out of sight, we can pray with greater focus and effectiveness. Quality time comes from quiet time, and quiet time comes from being alone with God.

Being alone for the sake of having quality time with someone reminds me of one time I went fishing with my boys. That time we didn't catch any fish, but we did catch a snail and a wood tick. Thankfully, we did not catch a cold! It was very quiet with just the three of us. As a parent, I coveted this time with my sons. Since we were not catching anything, I considered changing our location. As I was checking to see if we could get a canoe, I thought about how spending time with my boys was so much more important than actually catching fish. This was quality time with my sons, and we were able to break away and have a great time together. It was a quality time because it was a quiet time. Without the distractions of everyday life, we had a wonderful time together – even if the fish were not biting.

Sometimes our lives need to be more reflective; we need more quiet time with our Lord. This is why we need to have a place where we can get alone and focus – like a closet.

Our previous office building was an odd-shaped building. After we bought it, we remodeled it and cut some corners to make the rooms square. This remodeling resulted in one small area off the conference room that I had designated as my prayer closet. There, I was isolated from everybody, with just enough room to turn around. This little room was a place dedicated to focused prayer.

My friend Gary Miller wrote in a blog post, "Getting alone with God often requires getting away from others."[21] This is what

Jesus did in the wilderness and on the mountain. This is what Jesus said we should do in our closets. We simply must have times when we get away from others and give God our complete focus.

We must ask ourselves, "Where can we go for quietness? Where can we go to have our private communion with God in the midst of our busy lives?" It does not necessarily have to be in a closet, but it does need to be in a place where we are separated from other people and other distractions.

THE PATTERN OF FOCUSED PRAYER

Jesus exhibited a pattern of focused prayer throughout His life. Let us learn from His pattern of prayer.

SILENCE VERBAL DISTRACTIONS

And the apostles gathered themselves together unto Jesus, and told him all things, both what they had done, and what they had taught. And he said unto them, Come ye yourselves apart into a desert place, and rest a while: for there were many coming and going, and they had no leisure so much as to eat. And they departed into a desert place by ship privately.
Mark 6:30-32

Vance Havner wrote about the above passage stating this: "If we don't come apart, we will come apart."[22] Burnout is a very real affliction. As the world demands more and more from us, we must have time to get away, and to truly get away, we must silence our verbal distractions and not get caught up in the busyness of life. Friends, life is not going to slow down; it is only going to speed up. Unless we take deliberate action to silence those verbal distractions, they will only increase and choke off our focused time in prayer.

The power of our prayer will be determined in large degree by the privacy of our retreat.

Over the years I've had plenty of times when there would be constant interruptions. There would be a knock at the door, then a phone call, then a text message, another knock on the door with a lengthy conversation, and then I would get another phone call. Before long, all of my time would be gone. Nowadays, to add to the disruptions, my tablet is tied to my computer, which is tied to my phone, which is tied to my watch. My efforts to focus on prayer always seem to be an uphill struggle.

Sometimes we need to get away from all of that, silence all of the verbal distractions, silence our phones, turn off our emails, turn off text notifications, and put everything on "do not disturb." Sometimes we must say to others, "I'm going to take a little time, and I'm going to pray to my heavenly Father."

There is a pattern of focused prayer, and silencing all verbal distractions should be a key part of that pattern.

REDUCE VISUAL DISTRACTIONS

Not only must we silence verbal distractions, but we also need to reduce visual distractions. I know this sounds almost pointless because we pray with our eyes closed, right? Reducing distractions is probably one of the reasons why we pray with our eyes closed.

Prayer - Connecting with God

Many years ago, I was at a wedding and the person officiating the wedding said that they wanted to do something different that time. They said they wanted us to pray with our eyes open. Imagine 200 people looking at this person wondering about praying with their eyes open. I do not remember what we prayed about, but I do remember that someone's child was trying to start a fire with a candle in the middle of the table, and another person was pulling something out of their hair that looked like lice. This was not a reduction of visual distraction; it was an invitation to focus on everything but the prayer. To pray with focus, we must reduce our visual distractions as well as silence our verbal distractions.

Hebrews 12:2 speaks of "looking unto Jesus the author and finisher of our faith." How can we "look unto Jesus" when we are looking at everything around us? We need a place of prayer where we can go and not be distracted by visual stimuli.

How many times do we, when thinking about something, get distracted by something we see? Personally, I must have a clean desk before I can focus on study. My office must be clean too, or else I will be distracted by the stacks of papers, the full garbage can, and the dirty floor. Before I study, I make sure all of that is straightened out. Otherwise, I will find it difficult if not impossible to focus.

If you look at the desktop on my computer, you will notice there are no icons. All of my files and folders are neatly contained, and the desktop is completely blank. With all the visual distractions in my life, if I do not keep a clean desktop, then something will jump off the screen and say, "Joe, you know what, this is really important," and pretty soon the hour is gone.

We need to reduce our visual distractions. We need to look to Jesus, not to all of the stuff that is around us. R. A. Torrey said, "Much of our modern prayer has no power in it because there is no heart in it."[23] How can we put heart into prayer if we are constantly distracted by all of the sounds, visual stimuli, and crowds around us? How can we be focused on praying if the world around us is telling us that something else is more important? With all of the sounds and sights around, we must get away, eliminate those distractions, and think on the things we are praying about.

> *But mine eyes are unto thee, O GOD the Lord: in thee*
> *is my trust; leave not my soul destitute. Psalm 141:8*

To focus on prayer, we often need to be in solitude, but we also need to be silent. We need to be still. As Psalm 46:10 states, "Be still, and know that I am God: I will be exalted among the heathen, I will be exalted in the earth." We can be still and silent in the knowledge that God has everything under control. In that confidence we can focus on prayer and shut everything else out.

A busy life leads to many burdens. My propensity is just to get busier and busier and to do more and more because I think more means more. However, doing more things does not mean we are getting more done. Our lives are extremely busy because we allow more things into our lives that we have to do. We invite these burdens in with all of the phone calls, emails, and social media, as opposed to shutting them down for the sake of focused time with God.

Getting alone with God means following the pattern of getting away from other people and other distractions. Your life is so busy that you become burdened. You want to do so much and you feel guilty for not doing more. But even if you have to give some of this up, do not leave God behind. Focused time with God in prayer will enable you to accomplish so much more.

> *The effectual fervent prayer of a righteous man availeth much. James 5:16b*

> *I am the vine, ye are the branches: He that abideth in me, and I in him, the same bringeth forth much fruit: for without me ye can do nothing. John 15:5*

> *Come unto me, all ye that labour and are heavy laden, and I will give you rest. Matthew 11:28*

PRAYER POINTS

- When we pray, we must discipline ourselves to focus our attention on our prayer – and more importantly, on the One to whom we are praying.

- We need to step away, rise above the pressures of this life, and spend focused time alone with God.

- Quality time comes from quiet time, and quiet time comes from being alone with God.

- The power of our prayer will be determined to a large degree by the privacy of our retreat.

- We can be still and silent in the knowledge that God has everything under control. In that confidence we can focus on prayer and shut everything else out.

6

"Look well to it that you really pray, do not learn the language of prayer."

Charles Spurgeon

The Fervency of Prayer

A lady from our church had gone to Israel with us and bought an expensive necklace. One day, months later, she realized that her necklace was missing, and she could not remember the last time she had worn it. Having no idea where to look, she prayed and asked God to remind her of the last time she had it and to help her find it. She kept asking God over and over, every ten minutes or so, until finally, as she prayed once again, the Holy Spirit gently said to her, "This is what fervent prayer is." She was immediately convicted that while she had been fervently praying for her necklace, she had not been fervently praying for the salvation of her children. She would bring up her children in prayer once in a while, but she just could not stop praying about the necklace. She realized that the way she had been praying for her necklace was how she should have been praying for her children – passionately, feverishly, fervently.

Sadly, fervency is lacking in the prayer lives of many Christians. Too often, our prayers are casual, and we don't take them seriously. This results in us diminishing the importance of prayer. Then, the fervency of prayer is that much more diminished.

Instead of just letting our fervency diminish, we must ask ourselves a couple of questions regarding our prayer lives:

- **When was the last time we truly prayed with fervency?**
- **How seriously do we take our relationship with God?**

Think about this, for many of God's people, the Christian life has become a matter of routine. They may regularly go to church, and they may even read their Bibles and pray. But in reality, they are only performing rituals. They are keeping up appearances instead of cultivating a relationship. From the day God created Adam, man's relationship with God has been the key to everything else in life. It was always meant to be a fervent relationship and the center of one's existence, and communicating with God was a big part of that relationship.

So, how is our relationship with God? Would we describe it as fervent? Do we recognize the importance of prayer? When we pray, do we consider the fact that we are talking with the very Lord of the universe?

Have you ever had a conversation that, beforehand, you contemplated it and played it over and over again in your head because the conversation was very important? Perhaps it was a serious conversation that you needed to have with a friend or spouse, or perhaps it was a job interview for a position you really wanted. I remember one time when I preplanned a potential, short conversation with an important person: the president of the United States.

In 2017, I was invited to the Rose Garden at the White House on the National Day of Prayer. After I received my invitation, I would think of things like, "If I get a chance to meet the president or vice president, what am I going to say? How can I be an encouragement to them? There will only be about a hundred people there, so my chances are pretty good, right?" Then I would play out conversations with them. I thought of all sorts of things I could say, such as:

- "Keep up the good work."
- "Millions of Americans are praying for you."
- "I am committed to pray for you every day while you are in office."
- "The garden looks great!"

While I didn't meet them, I did get to speak to some of the staff. I may have had a potential opportunity to speak to the president or vice president, I thought of several conversations that never happened. Yet, that was only the president of the United States. A conversation with the Lord is much more significant than a conversation with any man.

In his book How to Pray, R. A. Torrey wrote, "Before a word of petition is offered, we should have the definite and vivid consciousness that we are talking to God."[24] Do we have this vivid consciousness of the presence of God when we pray? If we do, we will find that fervency in prayer comes almost naturally. Until we realize who we are talking to, we will never be able to pray fervently.

THE PARABLE OF A JUDGE

> *And he [Jesus] spake a parable unto them to this
> end, that men ought always to pray, and not to faint;
> Saying, There was in a city a judge, which feared not
> God, neither regarded man: And there was a widow
> in that city; and she came unto him, saying, Avenge
> me of mine adversary. And he would not for a while:
> but afterward he said within himself, Though I fear not
> God, nor regard man; Yet because this widow troubleth
> me, I will avenge her, lest by her continual coming she
> weary me. And the Lord said, Hear what the unjust
> judge saith. And shall not God avenge his own elect,
> which cry day and night unto him, though he bear long
> with them? I tell you that he will avenge them speedily.
> Nevertheless when the Son of man cometh, shall he
> find faith on the earth? Luke 18:1-8*

Notice the reason Jesus gave this parable: "Men ought always to pray, and not to faint." When it comes to prayer, fervency and fainting are opposites. The Greek word here translated "to faint" means "to be utterly spiritless."[25] That describes too many of our prayers.

Here, Jesus told the story of a judge who reluctantly gave in to the constant and fervent petitions of a widow. He was not a good judge; it was not a matter of justice with him. He cared for neither God nor man, only for his own ease and comfort. So, when this widow kept coming to him with such passion and persistence, he gave her what she wanted simply because he did not want to be bothered any longer. He saw that she would not be discouraged and would keep on asking until her request was granted. The point is, if an unjust judge will hear and reward such fervency, how much more will God hear the fervent pleadings of His own children? We see this in verse 7: "And shall not God avenge his own elect, which cry day and night?" That is a wonderful phrase, "which cry day and night." That is a good description of fervency.

Unlike the unjust judge, the Lord is full of compassion. He never wearies of our requests. "Pray without ceasing," the Scriptures tell us in 1 Thessalonians 5:17. God actually invites us to pray fervently because our fervency in prayer is one of the best indicators of our faith. Our faith pleases Him. We come to Him in full dependence, believing that as we diligently seek Him, we will be rewarded (Hebrews 11:6). Believing that God can answer our prayers gives us the confidence to keep asking Him until the prayers are answered. Fervency demonstrates faith.

Sometimes the problem is not whether we believe He can answer our prayers. We believe that He can, but we have doubts that He will. Do we believe at times that God is reluctant to hear and answer our prayers? Romans 8 should put this concept of God to rest:

> *He that spared not his own Son, but delivered him up*
> *for us all, how shall he not with him also freely give us*
> *all things? Romans 8:32*

Long before any of us were born, God already gave us His best. John 3:16 should never be far from our minds: "For God so loved the world, that he gave his only begotten Son, that whosoever believeth in him should not perish, but have everlasting life." If God gave us so much then, why would He not give us just a little now? All we need to do is ask, and we will never wear Him down with our requests. He is not like that unjust judge. He understands, and He cares!

> *For we have not an high priest which cannot be touched with the feeling of our infirmities; but was in all points tempted like as we are, yet without sin. Let us therefore come boldly unto the throne of grace, that we may obtain mercy, and find grace to help in time of need. Hebrews 4:15-16*

During the summer months, my two sons used to ask me if we could go fishing just about every day. Like every busy father, I said, "No, maybe next time." They kept coming back again and again, and I would say something like, "I'm sorry; we still can't go fishing. It's only been 15 minutes since the last time you asked!"

When they kept asking me, they were not wearing me down; rather, their fervency demonstrated that they believed I could and would indeed take them fishing. They believed in me, and I really liked that! Likewise, fervent prayer is a good indicator of our spiritual condition and our faith in God. Charles Spurgeon observed this truth when he said this:

> Prayer is the natural outgushing of a soul in communion with Jesus. Just as the leaf and the fruit will come out of the vine-branch without any conscious effort on the part of the branch, but simply because of its living union with the stem, so prayer buds, and blossoms, and fruits out of souls abiding in Jesus.[26]

Going to God in prayer continually and fervently flows naturally from our abiding in Him, from having a right relationship with the Lord, and from having our faith properly placed in Him as the One who can give us exactly what we need. We cannot weary Him, and we give Him glory when we persist in heartfelt and fervent prayer. We must look at our own spiritual lives and see if we truly have faith, focus, and fervency when we pray to our Lord.

THE EXAMPLE OF A PROPHET

The effectual fervent prayer of a righteous man availeth much. Elias was a man subject to like passions as we are, and he prayed earnestly that it might not rain: and it rained not on the earth by the space of three years and six months. And he prayed again, and the heaven gave rain, and the earth brought forth her fruit. James 5:16b-18

For an example of fervent prayer, James points us to Elias (Elijah in the Old Testament). The prophet prayed that it would not rain, and the result was three-and-a-half years of total drought. When the time was right, he prayed that it would rain again. With that, the drought ended. We read this account in 1 Kings 17-18. Elijah did not have access to some special power that is not available to us. Rather, he simply went to God, and he earnestly, passionately, and fervently prayed. This we all can do.

Passionate prayer is powerfully productive. Elijah "was a man subject to like passions as we are." Did God do great things through him? Yes, but was this man better than we are? No. He was a normal, ordinary person. After the great victory in 1 Kings 18, it seems strange to see him in the very next chapter caving in to fear, discouragement, and pride. But we can certainly relate to that. Our lives are also full of ups and downs, aren't they? God did not answer Elijah's prayers because he was perfect.

Remember, in the Old Testament an individual was saved the same way as in the New Testament. It has always been "by grace . . . through faith . . . not of works" (Ephesians 2:8-9). But the Old Testament saints did not have something that we have: the Holy Spirit living in them. Elijah had the Holy Spirit's power upon him, and he was able to pray effectively. Yet, we are actually better off than he was because we have the Holy Spirit living in us.

> *What? know ye not that your body is the temple of the Holy Ghost which is in you, which ye have of God, and ye are not your own? 1 Corinthians 6:19*

We know God is everywhere. How deeply do we realize that He is always with us in such a personal sense? What is the basic purpose of a temple, after all, but as a place of worship and prayer – much prayer and fervent prayer?

When we read the account of Elijah, we see his fervency in prayer: "And Elijah went up to the top of Carmel; and he cast himself down upon the earth, and put his face between his knees" (1 Kings 18:42). Does this resemble our relationship with God? Do we have that kind of focus and fervency when we cry out to God? Do we, in a sense, cast ourselves down in front of the Lord? Do we place our face between our knees and beg God until He answers us? We ought to. Elijah did what we all should do, what we all could do, but what we all usually fail to do: passionately and fervently pray. Elijah simply was not going to give up praying until he got what he was asking for – in this case, rain. James used this man as an example when he told us, "The effectual fervent prayer of a righteous man availeth much" (James 5:16).

It is said that when asked for his secret to prayer, John Bradford answered this: "When I know what I want, I always stop on that prayer until I feel that I have pleaded it with God, and until God and I have had dealings with each other upon it."[27]

There are times in our lives when we pray more fervently than others. Perhaps we are ill, we have lost a job, or experienced some tragedy, and that is when we cry out to God day and night. Those are the times we beg Him until we hear a definitive answer. This fervency should define our whole prayer life, not just when we are in trouble.

I struggle in this area as well. Most of the times that I have prayed earnestly have been times of trials in my life. It is easy to pray fervently when things are going wrong. Yet, what about when times are good? Do we still pray fervently to God? Do we look for the perfect peace in our lives? Do we ever find that peace? Perhaps we pray for something fervently, even for just a short period of time, and God gives us perfect peace. It is wonderful when that overwhelming sense of peace comes.

> *Thou wilt keep him in perfect peace, whose mind is stayed on thee: because he trusteth in thee. Isaiah 26:3*

There have been times in my life when I have prayed so earnestly about a specific thing that God has given me that perfect peace – such peace that I feel the thing is as good as done and further prayer on it is not needed. There are times when we can stop praying for something because God gives us that peace. There are other times we need to pray and never stop praying until we have seen the answer – for instance, praying for someone in your life who does not know Christ as Savior. Never give up on that. The Lord is not willing that any should perish, so just keep praying to God again and again until that person gets saved or dies. Keep going to God.

There are things in our lives that we should continually seek God for – such as our spiritual growth. It is important that we are never satisfied regarding spiritual things. Never give up or grow weary praying in this area.

I will never be satisfied with my spiritual condition, my children's spiritual condition, or my wife's spiritual condition. I will continue to go to God and be fervent about these issues. As the Scriptures say, I must continue to pray about these matters.

Continue in prayer, Colossians 4:2

Continuing instant in prayer; Romans 12:12

When a problem occurs in our lives, do we go to God right away and say, "Lord, I need your help?" or do we say, "Well, I'll deal with this some other time." When something goes wrong, we must determine to pray right then because the Bible says to continue instant in prayer. We must continue by not giving up or leaving until we pray about the matter. We must be fervent and seek God on it.

R. A. Torrey wrote, "One of the great needs of the present day is men and women who will not only start out to pray for things, but pray on and on and on until they obtain that which they seek from the Lord."[28] Do we pray "on and on and on" until we obtain that which we seek from the Lord? Are we like the widow who continued to ask the judge to avenge her? Do we continue to seek God for an answer to prayer like Elijah? We must pray until our prayers have prevailed or until we have received peace.

God wants to hear from you. Keep praying about your burdens. Be as persistent and fervent as my kids were when asking to go fishing. Never be content or complacent with your communion with God. Look for opportunities to improve your prayer life, and even pray about your prayer life.

Finally, talk with God as a man talks to his friend. When you pray with fervency, there is no need to be excessively formal. You should be reverent, of course, but not stiff. As Spurgeon said, "Look well to it that you really pray, do not learn the language of prayer."[29] Some of the most excellent prayers come out of the mouths of children because they have not yet learned the "prayer language" we sometimes slip into. They just go to God and ask Him plainly, and they are consistent about it. They pray with tremendous fervency.

Remember, "The effectual fervent prayer of a righteous man availeth much" (James 5:16). Pray with genuine fervency, and you will be a prayer warrior with access to the power of God. There is much power in fervent prayer!

PRAYER POINTS

- We Christians lack fervency in our prayer lives because we take prayer less seriously than we ought.

- Until we realize who we are talking to, we will never be able to pray fervently.

- Believing that God can answer our prayers gives us the confidence to keep asking Him until the prayers are answered.

- Passionate prayer is powerfully productive.

- There are times when we can stop praying for something because God gives us peace. There are other times we need to pray and never be satisfied with that prayer until we have seen the answer.

7

"Any concern too small to
be turned into a prayer is
too small to be made
into a burden."

Corrie ten Boom

The Frequency of Prayer

In the summer of 2019, our church's lawn mower was stolen. Just prior to that, we had paid almost $800 for that mower to be repaired. I prayed for the mower to be returned, and months later, it was miraculously found and returned. But during those first couple of weeks, as I prayed, I began to question how I was praying.

"Lord, if we don't get the mower back, I pray that the mower breaks down; just punish this criminal! No... Lord, I'm glad I fixed the mower for him."

Do you ever pray like that? Do you ever question how you are praying or if you are praying for the right thing?

Those are certainly important questions, but the area in which most of us need to improve is not necessarily the content of our prayers. Rather, our great need is to increase the frequency of our prayers. We may sometimes pray incorrectly, but all too often we pray too little. We must keep in mind that our communication is with the almighty God who is able to do anything, regardless of how we articulate our prayers. Because He loves us, He wants to hear from us often.

Communicating often with someone you love is very important to the relationship. You make it a priority. There are Christians who say, "I don't have an intimate relationship with the Lord, so I just don't pray very often." However, a lack of prayer is generally due to a lack of priority. When your life becomes more Christ-centered, you will pray more. The reverse is also true: when you pray more, your life becomes more Christ-centered. When your priorities in life are right, your prayer life will be strong, and when your prayer life is strong, your priorities will be right.

Along with the other qualities we are discussing in this book, a strong prayer life is characterized by frequency. What do the Scriptures have to say about how often we should be praying?

PRAY ALWAYS

In Ephesians 6, the Apostle Paul gives us specific instructions on how to be strong in the Lord and withstand the devil's attacks.

> *Finally, my brethren, be strong in the Lord, and in the power of his might. Put on the whole armour of God, that ye may be able to stand against the wiles of the devil. Ephesians 6:10-11*

Ephesians 6:12-17 goes on to describe this armor of God: the belt of truth, the breastplate of righteousness, the shoes of the gospel of peace, the shield of faith, the helmet of salvation, and the sword of the Spirit (the Word of God). We are commanded to put on the armor and be prepared, and then in verse 18, another command is given:

Praying always with all prayer and supplication in the Spirit, and watching thereunto with all perseverance and supplication for all saints; Ephesians 6:18

Why must we pray when we are armed? In a very real sense, prayer and watchfulness hold the armor in place. In the garden just before His arrest, Jesus told His disciples, "Watch and pray, that ye enter not into temptation: the spirit indeed is willing, but the flesh is weak" (Matthew 26:41). Proverbs 21:31 reminds us, "The horse is prepared against the day of battle: but safety is of the LORD." We should do everything we can to be prepared by putting on the whole armor of God. We should have all of the pieces in place to help us stand against the devil's attacks. But even with all of our preparation, we must pray to our real Protector. "Safety is of the LORD."

Notice that the prayer is to be "for all saints." Every one of us is under attack; all of us need God's protection. Sometimes, those whom the devil pursues are the ones who pursue the Lord the most. Have you experienced this in your life? As you begin to serve God and pray with more frequency, fervency, faith, and focus, the devil seems to double his efforts to get you off track.

Some of us may say, "Well, I don't really feel like praying right now," or "I'm not really in the mood to pray." I must confess that I have said that too. If everybody were honest with themselves and the Lord, we would all say that there are times when we do not feel like praying. There are times when it gets late, we are in a hurry, and we allow prayer to fall by the wayside. All of our prayer lives are lacking in some way because we give in to our human weaknesses; more accurately, we give in to sin.

One time I had to apologize to my kids: I had lied to them. It was horrible. My family and I were getting ready to eat dinner, and we were all rushing. Usually, I am the one who says, "Let's pray." I had thought about praying, but the food was so tempting that instead I just dug in and began to eat. My wife turned to me and said, "Should we pray?"

I said, "Yeah, I forgot." So, we prayed, and later I was overwhelmed with conviction. I had not forgotten to pray; the truth is that I had chosen not to pray. I had to go to my kids and tell them that I had lied to them.

There are times in our lives when we say, "I'm just too busy for prayer," or "I can't afford to spend time praying." This is not uncommon, but it is also untrue. We can't afford not to take the time to pray.

Sometimes we fail to pray because we think we are too busy; other times we fail to pray because we just do not feel like praying. Charles Spurgeon had an answer for this: "If your heart be cold in prayer, do not restrain prayer until your heart warms, but pray your soul unto heat . . . If the iron be hot then hammer it, and if it be cold hammer it till you heat it."[30] When you get to a point in your life where your spiritual iron is just not hot, hit it until you heat it. Pray when you don't feel like praying, but you must always pray. "Praying always with all prayer and supplication in the Spirit."

PRAY FOR EVERYTHING

We should pray always, and we should pray for everything. During one of our Wednesday prayer services, we began taking prayer requests. As I went around the room, I asked a four-year-old girl in our church if she had a prayer request. After some coaxing from her mom and dad, she said that she wanted to pray for her new, still unnamed, stuffed animal – a wild African dog. I do not recall specifically what the prayer request was other than that it was strange. I had never actually prayed for a stuffed animal before, but this was a great opportunity to show a little girl that we can pray for anything and everything. This is completely scriptural, according to Philippians 4:6: "Be careful for nothing; but in every thing by prayer and supplication with thanksgiving let your requests be made known unto God." I was glad this young girl had this prayer request because it showed me that she hadn't been influenced by us older Christians into believing that some things are not important enough to pray about. God wants to hear us talk to Him about everything.

In Philippians 4:6, "Be careful for nothing" means take no thought for anything or don't be anxious about anything. The Scripture is saying, "Worry about nothing; pray about everything." Verse 7 gives a promise to those who obey verse 6: "And the peace of God, which passeth all understanding, shall keep your hearts and minds through Christ Jesus." When we are anxious about something, we can go directly to God and have peace. Dr. John R. Rice wrote, "Anything that is big enough to worry about is big enough to pray about."[31]

We will have peace when we bring our burdens to the Lord, and we won't have peace as long as we insist on dealing with the burdens on our own. Until we yield to God, we will never be at peace. Many times we think, "I can get it done. I did it before, so why can't I do it this time?" and then we wonder why the burden is so heavy and why things go wrong. Yet, when we bring it to God and say, "Lord, please deal with this because I can't," we receive tremendous peace.

I remember when I was a kid, I would tell my dad about problems I was having, and he would usually respond, "I got this." A sense of peace would come over me as I told my dad my burden. Why? Because the problem was bigger than me, but it was not bigger than my dad. And no matter how much the devil tries to beat us down, no problem of ours is too big for God.

> *Ah Lord GOD! behold, thou hast made the heaven and the earth by thy great power and stretched out arm, and there is nothing too hard for thee: Jeremiah 32:17*

> *Behold, I am the LORD, the God of all flesh: is there any thing too hard for me? Jeremiah 32:27*

Knowing that nothing is too difficult for God, we are encouraged to go to Him for everything. As we pray more frequently, we will have more peace.

Corrie ten Boom said, "Any concern too small to be turned into a prayer is too small to be made into a burden."[32] Pray about any problem that is a burden to you, and God will give you peace because the problem is never bigger than Him.

David experienced peace many times in his life after he had prayed. Here is an example:

> *LORD, how are they increased that trouble me! many are they that rise up against me. Many there be which*

say of my soul, There is no help for him in God. Selah.
But thou, O LORD, art a shield for me; my glory, and the
lifter up of mine head. I cried unto the LORD with my
voice, and he heard me out of his holy hill. Selah. I laid
me down and slept; I awaked; for the LORD sustained
me. Psalm 3:1-5

Do you ever feel like those who trouble you are increasing, that the burdens keep getting heavier? That is exactly how David felt. After he prayed, he went to sleep, and when he woke, his burden was gone. He was no longer worried because the Lord had sustained him.

As the Lord answered David's prayers, David's faith grew. As he gained more faith, he prayed more fervently. As he prayed more fervently, he prayed more frequently. As he prayed more frequently, he had more prayers answered. This led David to have more faith! We see this cycle again and again, and it can become a reality in our own lives as well. As we see prayers answered, we grow in our faith. As we grow in our faith, we pray more fervently, and as we pray more fervently, we will pray more frequently. In the process, our faith widens, our fervency deepens, and our frequency increases. Our prayer life and our Christian life as a whole will prosper as we learn to pray about everything.

As we try to pray about everything, we may find that sometimes our prayers are rather vague. For instance, have you ever prayed or heard someone else pray, "Lord, bless all the missionaries"? Yes, we should want God to bless all of the missionaries; but in a practical sense, how would we know if God answered this prayer? We would not, and so it becomes apparent that our prayers should be both frequent and specific. Here are some suggestions for specific prayers:

PRAY FOR YOUR CHILDREN

I hope you pray for your children every day. Pray for them specifically by name, that they will come to know the Lord at an early age and serve Him faithfully. Pray for their daily needs, burdens, and challenges. If you have no children, then pray for someone else's children. Remember how much Jesus loved and valued children: "But Jesus said, Suffer little children, and forbid them not, to come unto me: for of such is the kingdom of heaven" (Matthew 19:14).

PRAY FOR YOUR MARRIAGE

If you are married, pray for all sorts of things concerning your marriage, but pray specifically that you can grow closer together. Pray for the strength of your marriage. If you are not married, pray for other people's marriages – they need it.

PRAY FOR YOUR GOVERNMENT

Pray for godly leaders within government and that they would be sensitive to the Holy Spirit's leading. Pray that they would not quench or grieve the Spirit, but that they would yield to His work. In 1 Timothy 2:1-2, Paul tells us, "I exhort therefore, that, first of all, supplications, prayers, intercessions, and giving of thanks, be made for all men; For kings, and for all that are in authority; that we may lead a quiet and peaceable life in all godliness and honesty."

PRAY FOR YOUR CHURCH AND YOUR PASTOR

I receive many text messages, but I especially appreciate those that say, "Pastor, I am praying for you this morning." You have no idea how that blesses and encourages me. During your devotional time, be sure to pray for your church and your pastor.

The list could go on and on. With so many people who need our prayers, there is no excuse not to pray frequently.

PRAY WITHOUT CEASING

We may ask, "How often should we pray? How frequent is frequent enough?" One of the clearest commands in Scripture regarding prayer comes from 1 Thessalonians 5:17: "Pray without ceasing." We are to have a continual dialogue with God all the time.

It becomes much easier to pray without ceasing when we realize how totally dependent we are on God. Have you ever considered that God literally gives us every breath and every heartbeat? Our prayer should be just as natural – and just as necessary – as the beating of our heart and our breathing. Jonathan Edwards put it this way: "Prayer is as natural an expression of faith as breathing is of life."[33]

The more we depend on God, the more frequently we will communicate with Him. At the time I am writing this book, my kids are dependent on me for food, shelter, and clothing. Since they are dependent on me, they come to me frequently.

"Dad, I need this," they will say. As they grow up and begin to become more self-sustaining, they will not depend on me as much. As a result, we will communicate less because they will need me less.

It is the same way in the Christian life. When we believe that we have a situation figured out and under control, we are not going to pray to God as we should. We come to think we are self-sustaining, and in this we make a grave mistake. Jesus said, "Without me ye can do nothing" (John 15:5).

While "Pray without ceasing" is short and to the point, notice the very next verse. 1 Thessalonians 5:18 says, "In every thing give thanks: for this is the will of God in Christ Jesus concerning you." Pray and give thanks. These two commands are connected. As we are to pray without ceasing, it could be said that we should also give thanks without ceasing. Thanklessness comes from an illusion of self-sufficiency, while thankfulness comes from a genuine dependency on God.

I came across a story in a book by Charles Spurgeon called Encouraged to Pray. May this account encourage you to keep your prayer going with God.

> A missionary some years ago, returning from Southern Africa, gave a description of the work which had been accomplished there, through the preaching of the gospel, and among other things he pictured a little incident of which he had been an eye-witness. He said that one morning he saw a converted African chieftain sitting under a palm tree with his Bible open before him. Every now and then he cast his eyes on his book and read a passage, and then he paused and looked up a little while, and his lips were seen to be in motion. Thus he continued alternately to look down on the Scriptures and to turn his eyes upward towards heaven. The missionary passed by without disturbing the good man, but a little while after he mentioned to him what he had seen, and asked him why it was that sometimes he read,

and sometimes he looked up? The African replied, – "I look down to the book, and God speaks to me, and then I look up in prayer, and speak to the Lord, and in this way we keep up a holy talk with each other."[34]

Is that the reality of your life? Do you have a continued "holy talk" with the Lord throughout your day? Think about how a day of "pray without ceasing" might go:

You walk outside in the morning, get a breath of fresh air, and say, "Thank You, Lord." Then you get into your car and say, "Thank You, Lord." Then you look down at your gas gauge and say, "Wow, Lord, I hope I can make it to the gas station!" When you get to the gas station, you say, "Thank You, Lord!" You then look over and pray that the gas is cheap. You see that the gas is cheap and say, "Thank You, Lord." Then you say, "Lord, I really need to make this meeting at work, and I must be there by 8:15. I pray, Lord, that I make it on time."

Maybe you show up at 8:17 and say, "Lord, thank You that I didn't get into an accident. I appreciate that very much. Even though I'm a little late, I hope they are okay with it." You get inside, and your boss is raging. You say, "Lord, I pray he isn't angry with me." You realize he is angry at you, and you pray, "Lord, give me peace." He then gives you peace, and you say, "Thank You, Lord, for that."

You go on to your next meeting, and something similar happens. Perhaps later you walk by someone and say, "Lord, this person needs a hand; I'm going to give this person some help. I just pray that You will give me the right words, and that I will be able to talk to this person."

You help them, and they say, "Thank you," and you say, "Well, praise God for that. I'm so glad I could help." Then you pray, "Thank You, Lord."

Is this the tone of your day? Do you have ongoing communion with God, or do you only seek Him when there is something that you cannot handle? I hope you have a conversation with the Lord all day long. Constantly pray and thank God for all He does for you. Pray always. Pray about everything. Pray without ceasing. According to the Word of God, you cannot pray too frequently.

PRAYER POINTS

- Our great need is to increase the frequency of our prayers. We may sometimes pray incorrectly, but all too often we pray too little.

- When your priorities in life are right, your prayer life will be strong, and when your prayer life is strong, your priorities will be right.

- We will have peace when we bring our burdens to the Lord; we will have no peace as long as we insist on dealing with the burdens on our own.

- Our prayer life, and our Christian life as a whole, will prosper as we learn to pray about everything.

- Our prayer should be just as natural – and just as necessary – as the beating of our heart and our breathing.

8

"Is there too much of me
and too little of others in
my prayers?"

Oswald Chambers

The Failure of Prayer

There are videos floating around social media that use the phrase "epic fail." Typically, this phrase is used with people involved in extreme sports, such as:

- A snowboarder crash-lands a jump.
- A skateboarder jumps on a rail, loses balance, and falls off.
- A surfer is toppled by a wave.

At the end of the video, the phrase "epic fail" appears on the screen. Unfortunately, when it comes to our prayers, we sometimes have epic fails too.

Although there are other reasons which we will discuss, the biggest reason our prayers fail is simply because we fail to pray. If we do not pray, why should we expect our prayers to be answered?

For those who do pray, I suspect that the main reason few prayers are answered is because few prayers are offered. This goes back to the matter of frequency in prayer. As Oswald Chambers put it, "Prayer seems like such a small thing to do. . . . We tend to pray as a last resort . . . when there is nothing else we can do."[35] It seems that oftentimes we only pray when we run out of other options.

What a shame that we pray so little to a God who can do so much! The Apostle Paul reminded us that our God is "able to do exceeding abundantly above all that we ask or think" (Ephesians 3:20). How much more could He do in our lives, if we would only take the time to ask?

Aside from our failing to pray at all, or our failure to pray very much, most of our epic fails in prayer boil down to two main problems: we fail to pray right, or we fail to live right. James expresses it in this way:

> From whence come wars and fightings among you? come they not hence, even of your lusts that war in your members? Ye lust, and have not: ye kill, and desire to have, and cannot obtain: ye fight and war, yet ye have not, because ye ask not. Ye ask, and receive not, because ye ask amiss, that ye may consume it upon your lusts. Ye adulterers and adulteresses, know ye not that the friendship of the world is enmity with God? whosoever therefore will be a friend of the world is the enemy of God. James 4:1-4

- "Ye have not, because ye ask not" – We fail to pray at all.
- "Ye ask amiss, that ye may consume it upon your lusts" – We fail to pray right.

- "Whosoever therefore will be a friend of the world is the enemy of God" – We fail to live right.

WE FAIL TO PRAY RIGHT

Some years ago, U.S. News funded a poll conducted by an organization called Beliefnet® to learn more about why, how, where, and when people pray. Here are a few of the statistics from their research:

- About 40% of the respondents said their prayers were answered often.
- About 1.5% said that their prayers were never answered.
- About 67% of people said that when their prayers were not answered, it was because their prayers did not fit God's plan.[36]

Most people said that when their prayers were not answered, they believed it was because their prayers were not according to God's will. Essentially, what they said is that they did not pray right. They felt that if they had prayed right, God would have responded.

How do we avoid failure in prayer? First, by simply being faithful to pray, but then, by learning how to pray. "The effectual fervent prayer of a righteous man availeth much" (James 5:16). Effectual prayers are answered prayers – they achieve their object; they bring victory. We need to pray with faith, focus, fervency, and frequency. We need to pray the way God tells us to pray.

Is there a certain way that we should pray? Is there a formula? Yes, there is, and I will address that in the next chapter. For now, notice the reasons we do not pray right.

WE WORSHIP THE WRONG GODS

> *Ye lust, and have not: ye kill, and desire to have, and*
> *cannot obtain: ye fight and war, yet ye have not,*
> *because ye ask not. James 4:2*

Lust and ungodly desires lead to crime and war; we see it all around us. Yet in a sense, we all tend to worship the gods of stuff. When we move to a new home, and of necessity shed some of our possessions, we realize that we should move more often because we accumulate so much! We live in a culture that endorses covetousness; have you ever heard the expression, "He who dies with the most toys, wins"? Romans 1 is very plain about this greedy culture of ours and its consequences:

> *For the wrath of God is revealed from heaven against*
> *all ungodliness and unrighteousness of men, who*
> *hold the truth in unrighteousness; . . . Who changed*
> *the truth of God into a lie, and worshipped and served*
> *the creature more than the Creator, who is blessed for*
> *ever. Amen. Romans 1:18,25*

Are we not part of a society that is more excited about the things that are created than the One who created those things? We all have a tendency to want instant gratification through immediate pleasures, and as a result, we worship the wrong gods – the gods of stuff.

People "fight and war" to get what they want so they will have something that nobody else has. It is a matter of pride. That is why they want the latest and greatest products available, such as the newest smartphone, a better car, or a bigger house. The competition never ends.

Years ago, as my dad and I were driving by a junkyard, he pointed toward the cars and said, "At one point in time, every one of those cars was somebody's dream." How long will it be before our dream of the new iPhone®, the new car, or the new house fades away? Just that quickly, we will be left looking for another dream. This approach to life is called hedonism. Hedonism is the belief that the pursuit of pleasure and possessions is the primary goal of living.

When we indulge in this way of thinking, our main goal is to be happy. Our prayer life is distorted because we focus on ourselves instead of on God. We will not pray right if we are just focused on pleasure and our attitude is, "I just want it for me." This attitude results in our expecting the temporal gods of stuff to fulfill our eternal needs. When those temporary things lose their attraction, rust out, or fall apart, we feel like we must go and get more because those things did not satisfy us. Because we worship the wrong gods, we ask for the wrong things: things that just make us feel good, and these things never last.

Hell and destruction are never full; so the eyes of man are never satisfied. Proverbs 27:20

Our eyes just keep wanting more! As for myself, I can never have enough guns. Because I had acquired so many guns, I had to get a nice gun safe. Now that I have this huge gun safe, I need more guns to fill it. I think, "There is plenty of space for another gun. What should I get?" However, "The eyes of man are never satisfied." The temporal things of this world can become overwhelming. When we take our eyes off the Lord, we will lust, kill, desire, fight, and war for the very things that will ultimately destroy us.

When we pray, we must make sure we are not praying to the wrong gods and not expecting eternal results from something that is temporal. The world will pass away, so it cannot produce anything that provides lasting happiness.

> *And the world passeth away, and the lust thereof: but*
> *he that doeth the will of God abideth for ever.*
> *1 John 2:17*

WE PRAY FOR THE WRONG GOODS

> *Ye ask, and receive not, because ye ask amiss, that ye*
> *may consume it upon your lusts. James 4:3*

Our prayers may fail because we pray to the wrong gods and secondly, because we pray for the wrong goods. How many times have we asked for something that only benefits us individually? How many times have we tried to justify to God why He should give us what we ask for, when we know full well that our prayer is basically a selfish prayer? Do we pray with the right motives, or are we asking for things so we can consume them upon our lusts?

This goes back to the 67% of people who, when their prayers were not answered, believed that their prayers were not in God's plan. Here are some examples of prayers that we may be tempted to pray with a wrong motive. The prayers themselves are good prayers, but the motives could potentially be wrong.

- Prayer: Lord, I pray for my wife. I pray that she would be more spiritual.

  Potential Motive: If she is more spiritual, she'll be nicer to people, and right now she's not very nice to me.

- **Prayer: Lord, I pray that my kids would read the Bible.**

  Potential Motive: There is much in the Bible about how they should treat others and how they should honor me as one of their parents.

- **Prayer: Lord, I pray that the congregation would be obedient in tithes and offerings.**

  Potential Motive: The church can afford a certain ministry that will benefit me or pay me more.

- **Prayer: Lord, I pray that people would come to church on Sunday.**

  Potential Motive: They need a church, and we'll be a bigger church if they come.

How often are our prayers tainted with our own passions? R. A. Torrey said, "A selfish purpose in prayer robs prayer of power."[37] Remember this: God knows us better than we know ourselves, and He knows whether or not we are praying for the right reasons. If we want God to work through our prayers, we must call on Him in truth, in total honesty. How many times do we pray with false pretenses while trying to appear to be spiritual?

So often our prayers are tainted with our desires, and we use our prayers for others as a mask for asking God for things we want. As Oswald Chambers asked, "Is there too much of me and too little of others in my prayers?"[38]

The LORD is nigh unto all them that call upon him, to all that call upon him in truth. Psalm 145:18

We should be asking God to search us as David did: "Search me, O God, and know my heart: try me, and know my thoughts:

And see if there be any wicked way in me, and lead me in the way everlasting" (Psalm 139:23-24).

When you pray, examine your motives. Give your prayer life some thought! Many people just pray without considering the underlying purpose of their prayers. If your motives are self-centered, ask God to help you change your prayers to reflect God-centered motives. Pray right: pray to the right God and for the right goods. This will help your prayers not to fail.

WE FAIL TO LIVE RIGHT

Not only do we fail to pray right, but we also fail to live right. Our failures to live right have much to do with our failures in prayer. We cannot live carelessly and expect to have our prayers answered. The prophet Isaiah made this very clear:

> Behold, the LORD'S hand is not shortened, that it cannot save; neither his ear heavy, that it cannot hear: But your iniquities have separated between you and your God, and your sins have hid his face from you, that he will not hear. Isaiah 59:1-2

When our prayers are not answered, we need to look to ourselves for the cause. Nothing is too hard for God. It is often our sin that blocks His blessing.

The Bible speaks of two specific scenarios which hinder our prayers from being answered: when we enjoy wickedness and when we do not honor our wives.

ENJOYING WICKEDNESS

> If I regard iniquity in my heart, the Lord will not hear me: Psalm 66:18

One commentator said that to regard iniquity in our hearts means "literally, 'see iniquity with pleasure.'"[39] The Bible says that "all have sinned" (Romans 3:23), but it is taking pleasure in the sin that makes the difference here. How often do we take pleasure in our sin? We may know our sin is not right and doesn't honor God, but we do not condemn it or walk away from it. When we do not see our sin the way the Lord sees it, we forfeit the blessing of answered prayer.

We should understand by now the consequences of sin. There are many sorrowful consequences to speeding, drinking, pornography, gambling, and other sins, but the greatest consequence of all is that we have offended God. How often do we engage in a sin against God and actually take pleasure in it? Do we think that our prayers will be heard?

> *Who knowing the judgment of God, that they which commit such things are worthy of death, not only do the same, but have pleasure in them that do them. Romans 1:32*

Those who love their sin more than they love their Savior cannot expect the Lord to hear their prayer. Spurgeon said, "Doubtless many lose power in prayer because their lives are grievous in the sight of the Lord, and he cannot smile upon them."[40] If we love the pleasure of sin, we cannot expect to have the favor of the Father.

NOT HONORING OUR WIVES

> *Likewise, ye husbands, dwell with them according to knowledge, giving honour unto the wife, as unto the weaker vessel, and as being heirs together of the grace of life; that your prayers be not hindered. 1 Peter 3:7*

Prayer - Connecting with God

One of the biggest reasons why men's prayers are not heard is because men do not honor their wives. We pray and ask God for His blessing on our family, but at the same time fail to honor the family He gave us. This dishonors God as well, and we should not be surprised that our prayers to God are hindered.

We must honor our wives. The Bible does not say, "Honor your wives when your wives are on their best behavior." That would be easy! It is easy to love the lovely. Instead, we are commanded to love our wives the way God loves us. This is a total love: an unconditional and sacrificial love.

> *Husbands, love your wives, even as Christ also loved the church, and gave himself for it; Ephesians 5:25*

With that in mind, wives, you need to treat your husbands right too – not just on Father's Day, or his birthday, but all the time. According to the Bible, you and your husband are "heirs together of the grace of life." It takes both of you.

I love to see a marriage where the husband and wife treat each other with great respect and honor: each being diligent to put the other one first. If each spouse is trying to put the other first, the worst thing that can happen is that there will be a competition to see who can treat the other better! What greater position could a couple be in than to try to outdo the kindness of the other?

In closing, let me give you two more verses that speak of failure in prayer.

> *For the eyes of the Lord are over the righteous, and his ears are open unto their prayers: but the face of the Lord is against them that do evil. 1 Peter 3:12*

This is a universal principle. This is not only for the husbands or only for the wives. This is for husbands, wives, sons, daughters, fathers, mothers, employers, employees, and everyone. Obedience to God is the way to get our prayers answered. Again, live right!

He that turneth away his ear from hearing the law, even his prayer shall be abomination. Proverbs 28:9

R. A. Torrey said, "If . . . we turn a deaf ear to His precepts, He will be likely to turn a deaf ear to our prayers."[41] Are you listening to God today? Are you praying right and living right? If you are, then you can expect that your prayers will succeed and not fail.

PRAYER POINTS

- The biggest reason our prayers fail to be heard is because we fail to pray.
- Our prayers fail when we fail to pray right and when we fail to live right.
- We fail to pray right when we worship the wrong gods and pray for the wrong goods.
- We fail to live right when we take pleasure in our sin and do not honor our spouses.
- If we love the pleasure of sin, we cannot expect to have the favor of the Father.

9

"I never knew a man getting a blessing in his own soul if he was not willing to forgive others."

D. L. Moody

The Formula of Prayer

When I was a boy, I did not enjoy school. I struggled especially with math. As I advanced in math I found, to my dismay, that I was required to memorize formulas. Formulas can be a scary thing! Even in my struggles though, I learned that formulas are useful: if you input the data properly, you will receive the desired result.

When it comes to prayer, there is a formula – not a potion or magic wand that guarantees you will get anything and everything you ask, but simply the teaching of the Word of God. If you do not follow this biblical formula, you will find yourself frustrated as you try to figure out why your prayers are not answered. However, if you do follow these simple steps, I believe they will be a tremendous benefit to your prayer life.

There are three basic components to this formula:

- The Need for Confession
- The Need for Calibration
- The Need for Confidence

THE NEED FOR CONFESSION

I will therefore that men pray every where, lifting up holy hands, without wrath and doubting. 1 Timothy 2:8

Powerful prayer is the result of a clean life. If we try to pray with unholy hands (not living right before God), how can we ask Him for things and expect a response? We must have pure hands when we go to the Lord in prayer. We have all sinned, as we know from the Scriptures, and we know that if we regard iniquity in our hearts the Lord will not hear us (Psalm 66:18). This is why there is a need for honest confession. It is the only way to be clean before the Lord and to gain His ear for our prayers.

If we confess our sins, he is faithful and just to forgive us our sins, and to cleanse us from all unrighteousness. 1 John 1:9

Do we want to be forgiven; do we want to be cleansed? Confession requires humility and humility stands in contrast to pride. How many times have we gone to somebody and admitted our wrongdoing? That's very humbling. We must confess our sins to have "clean hands, and a pure heart" (Psalm 24:4) before God, but pride often gets in the way.

The wicked, through the pride of his countenance, will not seek after God: God is not in all his thoughts. Psalm 10:4

When we are so arrogant and proud that we cannot confess our sins to God, there is a resistance and hesitation from God to bless us.

> *But he giveth more grace. Wherefore he saith, God resisteth the proud, but giveth grace unto the humble.*
> *James 4:6*

But James does give a blessed promise to the humble: "Humble yourselves in the sight of the Lord, and he shall lift you up" (James 4:10).

When we pray, do we want to encounter God's resistance or God's grace? The answer should be obvious. We deserve nothing good from God; all of His blessing comes from His grace. The key to grace and the key to answered prayer is humility before God. Humility will naturally lead to confession. It was for the prophet Isaiah when he saw the Lord "high and lifted up" (Isaiah 6:1). He was moved to cry out, "Woe is me! for I am undone; because I am a man of unclean lips, and I dwell in the midst of a people of unclean lips: for mine eyes have seen the King, the LORD of hosts" (Isaiah 6:5). When we see the Lord as He is, we will see ourselves as we are. We will be humbled and brought to confession, and we will have His forgiveness and His grace.

Have you humbled yourself before your God? If you have something in your life that you need to confess, ask God for forgiveness for your transgression against Him. If you want power in your prayer, if you want a formula for prayer that works, begin with confessing your sinfulness – right here, right now.

The beautiful thing about it all is that, because of Christ, we are invited into the presence of a loving heavenly Father. He loves to hear us pray, but we must come to Him on His terms. I remember complicated math formulas that had many brackets, parentheses, letters, and numbers. The formula of prayer is not complicated, but it begins with confession.

THE NEED FOR CALIBRATION

Just as a carpenter must check his work with a level and make corrections as necessary, if we want the Lord to hear and answer our prayers, then we need to align our lives with the will of God and the Word of God. Confession to God is the place to start – we cannot begin to make things right if we cannot admit we are wrong. Admitting we are wrong is the beginning of sensitivity toward spiritual things. We need to be rightly calibrated, both spiritually and scripturally.

SPIRITUAL CALIBRATION

Speaking to His disciples, Jesus said, "If ye abide in me, and my words abide in you, ye shall ask what ye will, and it shall be done unto you" (John 15:7). The context of this passage concerns the relationship between the Vine (Christ) and the branches (us). As the branch abides in the vine, it brings forth fruit. A branch lying on the ground cannot bear fruit; it has to be attached to the vine, its life source. The fruitfulness of the branch is determined by its faithfulness to abide in the vine. What a perfect illustration of the Christian's relationship with Christ! Answered prayer comes from a firm relationship with the One who can supply the answer to the prayer. If there is no abiding, there will be no fruit.

This explains why spiritual people have their prayers answered. They are spiritually calibrated. Spiritual calibration is simply walking in the Spirit and having a right relationship with the Lord. If you walk with the Lord, you will be spiritually calibrated. God asked His people this question through the prophet Amos: "Can two walk together, except they be agreed?" (Amos 3:3). The answer is no; we cannot walk with the Lord without being in agreement with Him. Agreement with God leads to answered prayer.

> *And whatsoever we ask, we receive of him, because we keep his commandments, and do those things that are pleasing in his sight. 1 John 3:22*

As we keep God's commandments and live to please Him, we can pray and have our prayers answered. God answers our prayers when we confess our sins, are sensitive to sin, and pray while abiding in Jesus. When we do these things, we calibrate ourselves spiritually.

SCRIPTURAL CALIBRATION

The idea of scriptural calibration is explained well by R.A. Torrey, who wrote, "If we would have power in prayer, we must be earnest students of His Word to find out what His will regarding us is, and then having found it, do it."[42] If we do not know God's Word, how can we know God's will? If we do not know God's Word, how can we know what to pray for?

While reading the Scriptures, I have often said to God, "Lord, I just need an answer on this thing." As I continued reading, I would come to a particular verse or passage and realize, "That's it! That's the answer I was looking for." God will speak to us, but we have to be paying attention. If we want the answers, we must go to the Person who has them and then listen to what He has to say. The answers we need are right there in God's Word. Scriptural calibration comes from studying the Bible, knowing God's will, and praying according to His will.

R.A. Torrey also stated that we must "feed the fire of our prayers with the fuel of God's Word."[43] How do we fuel our fire of prayer? By reading, studying, and memorizing God's Word. We must be calibrated spiritually and scripturally. This will allow us to know God's will for our lives.

It is easy to have our prayers answered when we are asking Him for what He already wants us to have. Being spiritually and scripturally calibrated, we can pray in a way that pleases God.

> *And whatsoever ye shall ask in my name, that will I do,*
> *that the Father may be glorified in the Son. If ye shall*
> *ask any thing in my name, I will do it. John 14:13-14*

Asking in Jesus' name is asking in the will of God, for His name's sake, and for His glory. If we ask God for something that is in His will, He will not deny us! I can look into the Word of God and say, "Lord, I know that You want me to be a good husband. I am praying that You would help me to be a good husband – not for my wife's sake, but for His name's sake. I want to bear a good testimony in Jesus' name." We must pray in His will and in His name, but we will never know what to ask for if we are not students of His Word.

Aside from being spiritually and scripturally calibrated, there are other things we must consider in the discussion of being calibrated for prayer. These include forgiveness and thanksgiving. Both of these are matters of the heart.

FORGIVENESS

In His Sermon on the Mount, Jesus taught on the subject of prayer and included this statement in His model prayer:

And forgive us our debts, as we forgive our debtors.
Matthew 6:12

On another occasion, He told His disciples this:

And when ye stand praying, forgive, if ye have ought against any: that your Father also which is in heaven may forgive you your trespasses. But if ye do not forgive, neither will your Father which is in heaven forgive your trespasses. Mark 11:25-26

As we go through life, sometimes others wrong us. We sometimes have a difficult time forgiving them. But Jesus made it very clear that we cannot ask for God's forgiveness and pray successfully if we ourselves are not willing to forgive. It takes humility to forgive others because in doing so we realize how often and how much we need forgiveness ourselves. As I have already stated, humility is the key to prayer, and God resists the proud. We must forgive those who have wronged us if we want God to answer our prayers.

You may be wondering, "What if they don't ask for forgiveness?" Forgive them anyway. Say something like this to God: "Lord, I'm going to forgive this person. They may never come to me, but I'm forgiving them because I don't want anything to stand in the way of my relationship with You."

D. L. Moody put it this way: "I never knew a man getting a blessing in his own soul if he was not willing to forgive others."[44] If you want to be blessed of God, you must be a forgiving person.

THANKSGIVING

> *Rejoice evermore. Pray without ceasing. In every thing give thanks: for this is the will of God in Christ Jesus concerning you. 1 Thessalonians 5:16-18*

> *Be careful for nothing; but in every thing by prayer and supplication with thanksgiving let your requests be made known unto God. Philippians 4:6*

If you pray and are not thankful when God answers, do you think that God will keep answering your prayers? If I give my children a ten-dollar bill, and they just grab it and say nothing, I would not be inclined to give them another one.

We need to pray with thanksgiving. There is always so much to be thankful for. We should say, "Thank You, God, for giving me this, and if I never get anything else, I can thank You for all eternity for what You have already given me." It is a good practice to write down all the things that God does for us, bring it out often, and say, "Thank You, Lord!"

Thankfulness is a key component of the formula for having our prayers answered. Without it, we cannot be properly calibrated with the Lord.

When I was on the police department, we had to calibrate (tune) our radar detectors. If we failed to tune them at the beginning of each shift, we would risk inaccurate readings resulting in speeding tickets the drivers could successfully fight in court. The radar had to be tuned so we could perform this part of our job properly. In the same way, we must calibrate ourselves spiritually, scripturally, with forgiveness, and with thanksgiving, because we will go "out of tune" and become misdirected in our prayer life.

Check your life right now for good calibration with the Lord. Are you walking with Him today, or are you running ahead or lagging behind Him? Calibrating your life just once a year on New Year's Day will not do. Calibration should be a constant concern for all of us.

THE NEED FOR CONFIDENCE

And this is the confidence that we have in him, that, if we ask any thing according to his will, he heareth us: And if we know that he hear us, whatsoever we ask, we know that we have the petitions that we desired of him. 1 John 5:14-15

When we have confessed our sin and are calibrated spiritually and scripturally, then we can and ought to pray with confidence that He will hear and answer. We can pray, "This is the will of God! I've looked at it in the Scripture, and I know this to be true. I am living a pure life in front of You, Lord, and You said that I can ask You for things with confidence." We can rest assured that God will always live up to His promises.

When we pray, we must believe that we will receive what we are asking for. This is part of the confidence that the Bible clearly tells us to have. When we go to God, we can pray in faith, knowing that we are asking for the things God wants to give us.

Therefore I say unto you, What things soever ye desire, when ye pray, believe that ye receive them, and ye shall have them. Mark 11:24

Many Christians pray with a lack of confidence. They are unsure that their requests are what God desires for them, so they waver.

They begin to ask themselves, "Does prayer work?" They prayed the wrong way and did not get an answer, so instead of changing the way they prayed, they eliminate prayer altogether.

If you are wavering in your prayers and see they are not answered, then take that as a verification the Bible is true! James 1:6-7 states, "But let him ask in faith, nothing wavering. For he that wavereth is like a wave of the sea driven with the wind and tossed. For let not that man think that he shall receive any thing of the Lord."

We must pray in confidence, knowing that God wants to give us what we are asking for. If you are praying in God's will, understand that what you are praying for has great value. Actually, He wants it more than we do. Jeremy Taylor said, "For, consider what a huge indecency it is, that a man should speak to God for a thing that he values not."[45]

If we are going to God, confessing our sins, calibrating our lives spiritually and scripturally, forgiving others, thanking God, and praying in confidence, we can know that our prayers will be answered based on the sure promises of God.

How are you living? How are you praying? What are you praying for? What are your motives when you pray? If your prayers are not answered, do not blame God. Instead, look to yourself. God is a really good God! He is not trying to hold something back from you. He wants only what is best for you. So always look to yourself for why your prayers are not answered.

For the LORD God is a sun and shield: the LORD will give grace and glory: no good thing will he withhold

*from them that walk uprightly. O LORD of hosts,
blessed is the man that trusteth in thee. Psalm 84:11-12*

The formula is simple: confession, calibration, and confidence. This is a formula that works because it is simply God's formula. A formula for math can be scary, but the formula for prayer is a wonderful thing!

PRAYER POINTS

- There are three basic components to the formula of prayer:

  The Need for Confession
  The Need for Calibration
  The Need for Confidence

- Powerful prayer is the result of a clean life.

- Spiritual calibration is simply walking in the Spirit and having a right relationship with the Lord.

- Scriptural calibration comes from studying the Bible, knowing God's will, and praying according to His will.

- Forgiveness and thankfulness are key components to having our prayers answered.

- As we meet God's conditions and apply God's formula, we can know that our prayers will be answered based on the sure promises of God.

10

"Your discouragement is really just a lack of God's nearness and assurance..."

John R. Rice

The Freedom of Prayer

There are few things as important to us as our freedom. We treasure freedom in all areas of life. We treasure all sorts of freedom: financial freedom, physical freedom, freedom to choose for ourselves. Nobody likes bondage.

If you have ever been stuck in the snow, you know how it feels to be freed. That moment your tires grab the pavement and get traction, you feel great! It is wonderful to be free because nobody likes to be stuck.

This desire for freedom is one of the reasons why prayer is such a wonderful thing. Prayer brings freedom. One of the greatest aspects of prayer is the freedom we experience when we spend time in prayer with God.

FREEDOM FROM OUR ANXIETY

Prayer gives us freedom from anxiety. Millions of people across the world, young and old, in all walks of life, experience worry and anxiety. Even God's people can easily become anxious and frustrated. For so many, this is a real struggle. Yet, as Christians, we can be free from worry! We are not supposed to worry about anything, and prayer is the key.

> *Be careful for nothing; but in every thing by prayer and supplication with thanksgiving let your requests be made known unto God. Philippians 4:6*

"Be careful for nothing" simply means do not be anxious (troubled with cares) about anything. The best way to release worry and anxiety is to go to God in prayer, because prayer brings freedom. Note the promise given in verse 7: "And the peace of God, which passeth all understanding, shall keep your hearts and minds through Christ Jesus." The peace of God – that is real freedom from care and anxiety.

God invites us to come to Him in prayer, and He freely offers us His peace. Many years ago, Charles Weigle wrote a song called, "No One Ever Cared for Me Like Jesus." Indeed, nobody cares for us like our Lord does. But just as it takes humility to confess sin, it takes humility to confess how much we need the Lord and to bring all of our cares to Him.

> *Humble yourselves therefore under the mighty hand of God, that he may exalt you in due time: Casting all your care upon him; for he careth for you. 1 Peter 5:6-7*

Worry accomplishes nothing, but prayer can accomplish everything because "with God all things are possible" (Mark 10:27).

This is the way to relieve our anxiety. When we experience the pressures of life, we can go to God and cast our cares on Him. Thank God He cares about us! In prayer, we can find freedom from anxiety.

JOY COMES FROM GOD

It is astounding to me how frequently we try to find joy in things that can never give joy. When we try to attain joy from material gain or pleasures, we come to realize that there is no lasting joy in those things. They actually do not relieve us from anxiety; instead, they create more anxiety. Why? Because possessions make life more complicated. Not only do we collect our possessions, but then we must preserve and protect them. Since these things do not really satisfy us, we find ourselves pursuing the next thing while at the same time dealing with the things we already have. It is no wonder possessions create anxiety! True joy never comes from anything other than God.

> *Thou wilt shew me the path of life: in thy presence is fulness of joy; at thy right hand there are pleasures for evermore. Psalm 16:11*

Apart from the presence of God, we can never have full joy. "Fulness of joy" is not some cheap, halfhearted, fragile joy. It is a full joy that affects every area of our lives. When we seek God, talk with Him, cast our cares upon Him, and bring our problems to Him, we find freedom from anxiety. The closer we get to God, the deeper the joy and the greater the pleasure.

John R. Rice said, "Your discouragement is really just a lack of God's nearness and assurance,"[46] and I certainly can attest to that statement. When I find I have lost my joy in the Lord, when I am worried, discouraged, and weighed down with burdens, it is usually because I have neglected prayer. The only thing that can truly give encouragement is meeting with the Lord. This is why we find joy in the Lord and freedom from anxiety when we pray.

In any situation, prayer is truly the best thing we can do. It should be a top priority in our lives. It seems like we always resort to prayer last, but we should be eager to go to our heavenly Father and talk to Him about everything. When we are anxious, worried, and feeling helpless and hopeless, the first thing we must do is go to God and pray. God is the Source of joy – so right at the start, go to the Source.

We experience joy when we have a real conversation with God – when we talk to God in prayer and God talks to us through His Word. This is what the Psalmist meant when he said, "in thy presence is fulness of joy." When we are in the presence of God, God gives us joy.

GRACE COMES FROM GOD

Praise God we can pray in times of difficulty! When we are going through a trial and we know we need the grace of God (His favor and loving-kindness) to get through it, prayer is the way to find that grace.

> *Let us therefore come boldly unto the throne of grace, that we may obtain mercy, and find grace to help in time of need. Hebrews 4:16*

How do we find grace to help us in our time of need? We come to God. That is God's solution for the trials we go through. But boldly? Yes, because we are invited!

> *Come unto me, all ye that labour and are heavy laden, and I will give you rest. Take my yoke upon you, and learn of me; for I am meek and lowly in heart: and ye shall find rest unto your souls. For my yoke is easy, and my burden is light. Matthew 11:28-30*

We can approach the Lord boldly and know that He will give us the grace we need. But keep in mind, "boldly" is not the same thing as "arrogantly." Spurgeon said, "We are to come boldly unto the throne of grace, yet always with submission in our hearts."[47] How often do we go boldly to the throne of grace without submission? How many times do we ask for things from God, and yet we do not yield ourselves to His will? Jesus set the example when He prayed in the garden, "Not my will, but thine, be done" (Luke 22:42). When we come boldly and yet submissively into His presence during our troubles, we can feel our burdens lifted. God gives us His grace, and we receive freedom from anxiety.

The Apostle Paul understood this. We do not know exactly what his problem was, but it seems to have been some kind of physical affliction. He called it "a thorn in the flesh." In 2 Corinthians 12, Paul tells us what he did and what he discovered:

> *For this thing I besought the Lord thrice, that it might depart from me. And he said unto me, My grace is sufficient for thee: for my strength is made perfect in weakness. 2 Corinthians 12:8-9*

When he prayed about his problem, Paul found that the grace of God was enough. Verse 9 goes on to say, "Most gladly therefore will I rather glory in my infirmities, that the power of Christ may rest upon me." He was happy to keep his problem as long as he had God's grace to deal with it.

All afflictions are not bad things. Why? Because they draw us to God.

In June of 2019, my wife had a cancer scare. After a routine mammogram, a spot was discovered. That put me on my knees in my closet, and I begged God, "Lord, may some good come out of this." I thank the Lord that the spot was benign. But do you know what happened because of that trial? I became closer to the Lord. I was humbled, and the Lord became very close to me because He is nigh to everyone who has a broken heart and contrite spirit.

> *The LORD is nigh unto them that are of a broken heart; and saveth such as be of a contrite spirit. Many are the afflictions of the righteous: but the LORD delivereth him out of them all. Psalm 34:18-19*

A good sculpture undergoes a lot of chiseling. A sculptor can look at a piece of marble and say, "I can make something out of this." Yet, when most of us look at the same piece, we just see a rock. When God looks at our lives, He says, "I can make something out of this." He sets in motion a plan to chisel off some of our rough edges, smooth us out, and make something beautiful. There may be some pain, but when God is done, we are going to look much more like Jesus.

How often do we feel like the problem is ours to deal with? We so easily forget the invitation, "come unto Me." We should say, "Lord, the problem is not mine to solve; I'm going to pray. I'm going to ask You, Lord, to help me." When we pray, we will find joy, we will find grace, and we will find freedom from our anxiety. It has been said many times, why worry when you can pray?

FREEDOM FROM OUR ABILITY

As human beings, and especially as we get older, we understand we have limitations. For myself, I know that I have some intellectual limitations, some physical limitations, and many others as well. These limitations can be discouraging, and we often feel weak and powerless. Yet, when we go to God and realize His abilities, we will find freedom from our own.

WE HAVE LIMITATIONS

Watch ye and pray, lest ye enter into temptation. The spirit truly is ready, but the flesh is weak. Mark 14:38

To whom did Jesus address this? He said it to the disciples in the garden. They all thought they were strong and loyal men and had boasted that they would never deny Him. They would soon find out differently. Like them, we will not find the power of God until we come to the end of ourselves and understand how weak our flesh is. Often God puts us in a place to help us realize that we are powerless. When we pray as we should, we say in our hearts, "Lord, it's not my ability that counts, but Yours." Without prayer, we are limited to our own feeble abilities. Our flesh is weak, so we must watch and pray.

GOD HAS NO LIMITATIONS

Ah Lord GOD! behold, thou hast made the heaven and the earth by thy great power and stretched out arm, and there is nothing too hard for thee: Jeremiah 32:17

Call unto me, and I will answer thee, and shew thee great and mighty things, which thou knowest not. Jeremiah 33:3

I am so glad that when we pray we come to a God who has unlimited ability. We can be free from our anxieties and our abilities because God has no limitations. Think about it: He created the universe and everything in it, He keeps track of it all, and yet He pays attention to every sparrow that falls and every hair on our head (Matthew 10:29-30). He has all knowledge and all power and is everywhere present. As if that were not enough, He is love (1 John 4:8). We can pray with freedom in the assurance that He has everything we need and delights to give it to us.

Prayer gives us the ability to surpass our own limitations and tap into God's strength – strength that we cannot have unless we call on Him. This is why Paul could say, "When I am weak, then am I strong" (2 Corinthians 12:10). It may sound like a paradox to say that weakness provides strength, but it is the realization of our weakness that causes us to stop trusting our abilities and instead to trust fully in God. When we pray and depend on Him, we are strong because He gives us His strength.

Notice how these two concepts are woven together: there is no greater relief from anxiety than when we are trusting in God's ability. When we are no longer anxious, and we are depending on

God, we will find our spirits lifted. When we pray and cast all of our care on Him, we will find that our care is gone!

We sometimes say, "All we can do is pray," but the truth is that we should be shouting, "Praise God – all we can do is pray!" There is truly nothing better to do than pray. We are not qualified to provide the solution because, really, we are part of the problem. God has the solution, and more than that, God is the solution. We should not be discouraged when all we can do is pray because through prayer we can have freedom from anxiety and freedom from our ability. We are at the point where God will intervene because the only thing we can do is pray.

In closing, as you pray, remember the following truth and keep it close to your heart:

> *He that spared not his own Son, but delivered him up for us all, how shall he not with him also freely give us all things? Romans 8:32*

Since God gave you the best He has, why would He not give you everything else you need? You can see that God has put His relationship with you above all else, and you too need to put that relationship first in your life. Pray to your Lord with faith, focus, fervency, and frequency. When you do, you will experience the freedom that prayer brings.

Thank you for taking the time to read this
book. Now, take time to pray!

PRAYER POINTS

- One of the greatest aspects of prayer is the freedom we experience when we spend time in prayer with our God.

- God invites us to come to Him in prayer, and He freely offers us His peace.

- God is the Source of joy – so right at the start, go right to the Source.

- In our trials, God's grace is available to us through prayer.

- Our flesh is weak, and so we must watch and pray.

- When we pray and depend on Him, we are strong because He gives us His strength.

APPENDIX 1
STUDY GUIDE

CHAPTER 1
A RELATIONSHIP WITH GOD

1. What is the most important element of any relationship?

2. How does God communicate with us?

3. What shows that we lack proper understanding of prayer?

4. Describe the difference between informative knowledge of God, intellectual knowledge of God, and intimate knowledge of God.

5. As we fall in love with the Lord and come to know Him in an intimate way, what will naturally follow?

ANSWERS
A RELATIONSHIP WITH GOD

1. In any relationship, communication is the most important element.

2. God communicates with us through His Word and through the Holy Spirit.

3. "The fact that we do not make time to pray reveals that we lack a proper understanding of prayer."

4. Answers may vary but should include these ideas: Informative knowledge is the basic knowledge everyone has, intellectual knowledge is an accumulation of facts, and intimate knowledge is a personal experience with God.

5. "As we fall in love with the Lord and come to know Him in an intimate way, our obedience will naturally follow."

CHAPTER 2
THE FUNCTION OF PRAYER

1. The function of prayer can be described as what three things?

2. According to Hebrews 4:16, how can we "obtain mercy, and find grace to help in time of need"?

3. Give a definition of "communion."

4. Considering the command to "pray without ceasing," how can we be in a constant state of prayer?

5. What did Dr. John R. Rice say was our greatest sin and the cause of all our failures?

ANSWERS
THE FUNCTION OF PRAYER

1. The function of prayer can be described as three things: communication with God, communion with God, and a command from God.

2. Let us therefore come boldly unto the throne of grace, that we may obtain mercy, and find grace to help in time of need. Hebrews 4:16

3. Answers may vary but should include the concept of "the sharing or exchanging of intimate thoughts and feelings."

4. "We can be in a constant state of prayer in our subconscious where we continually think about our heavenly Father and talk with Him."

5. He wrote, "My greatest sin, and yours, is prayerlessness. My failures are all prayer-failures."

CHAPTER 3
THE FOUNDATION OF PRAYER

1. Explain the concept, "Just as the foundation of a building and the foundation of life are vital, the foundation of our prayers is also vital."

2. List some characteristics of God that are foundational to His character and to our understanding of who He is.

3. Keeping the alliteration in mind, what words were used to describe God's love, goodness, and mercy?

4. Complete this sentence: "We must have a right view of _____, for this is just as foundational to prayer as having a right view of our Savior."

5. Despite your failures, what allows you to have a wonderful relationship with God?

ANSWERS
THE FOUNDATION OF PRAYER

1. Answers may vary but should include this idea: "A good foundation is important to the integrity of a building. A poor foundation will eventually cause the whole structure to fail. . . . Before we even start to pray, we must remember who we are and to Whom we are praying; these are foundational matters."

2. "God's love, God's goodness, and God's mercy are foundational to His character and to our understanding of who He is."

3. God's love is limitless, God's goodness is great, and God's mercy is measureless.

4. "We must have a right view of ourselves, for this is just as foundational to prayer as having a right view of our Savior."

5. God's faithfulness allows you to have a wonderful relationship with your heavenly Father.

CHAPTER 4
THE FAITH OF PRAYER

1. Complete this sentence: "The more we _____ God, the more eager and effective our prayers will be to God."

2. According to Hebrews 11:6, what must we have and what must we do to please God?

3. In Scripture, what do we usually find coupled with faith?

4. According to Romans 10:17, faith is developed through learning and understanding _____.

5. List three ways to increase your faith.

ANSWERS
THE FAITH OF PRAYER

1. "The more we believe God, the more eager and effective our prayers will be to God."

2. But without faith it is impossible to please him: for he that cometh to God must believe that he is, and that he is a rewarder of them that diligently seek him. Hebrews 11:6

3. "We usually find faith and action coupled together in Scripture."

4. So then faith cometh by hearing, and hearing by the word of God. (Romans 10:17)

5. Faith is developed through learning and understanding the Scriptures.

   "Get to know God's Word better."
   "Remember what He has done."
   "Get out of His way."

CHAPTER 5
THE FOCUS OF PRAYER

1. On what and on whom must we focus when we pray?

2. What did Jesus mean when He said we should pray in our closets?

3. Describe two types of distractions that may keep us from focusing on prayer.

4. According to Psalm 46:10, we are to "be _____," and know that He is God.

5. What will you need to do in order to spend focused time with God in prayer?

ANSWERS
THE FOCUS OF PRAYER

1. "When we pray, we must discipline ourselves to focus our attention on our prayer – and more importantly, on the One to whom we are praying."

2. "When we pray, we need to get alone with God so we will not be tempted to seek praise from men for our pretty prayers. Alone and out of sight, we can pray with greater focus and effectiveness."

3. We must silence verbal distractions and reduce visual distractions.

4. Be still, and know that I am God: I will be exalted among the heathen, I will be exalted in the earth. Psalm 46:10

5. Answers may vary.

CHAPTER 6
THE FERVENCY OF PRAYER

1. What is meant by "fervency" in prayer?

2. Complete this sentence: "Until we realize _____, we will never be able to pray fervently."

3. In the parable of the unjust judge, what was the key to the widow's successful petition?

4. According to James 5:16 and the example of the prophet Elijah, what kind of prayer gets results?

5. List some particular things in your life for which you ought to pray fervently.

ANSWERS
THE FERVENCY OF PRAYER

1. Answers may vary but should include the concepts of passion, persistence, and earnestness.

2. "Until we realize who we are talking to, we will never be able to pray fervently."

3. "So, when this widow kept coming to him with such passion and persistence, he gave her what she wanted simply because he did not want to be bothered any longer. He saw that she would not be discouraged and would keep on asking until her request was granted."

4. "The effectual fervent prayer of a righteous man availeth much." James 5:16

5. Answers may vary, but could include the salvation of loved ones and spiritual growth for yourself and others.

CHAPTER 7
THE FREQUENCY OF PRAYER

1. Complete this sentence: "A lack of prayer is generally due to a lack of _____."

2. Although it is true that when your life becomes more Christ-centered, you will pray more, what else is true?

3. Why must we pray to God even after we are prepared with the whole armor of God?

4. According to Philippians 4:6-7, what promise is given to those who take everything to God in prayer?

5. What is the clear command given in 1 Thessalonians 5:17 concerning the frequency of our prayers?

ANSWERS
THE FREQUENCY OF PRAYER

1. "A lack of prayer is generally due to a lack of priority."

2. "The reverse is also true: when you pray more, your life becomes more Christ-centered."

3. "In a very real sense, prayer and watchfulness hold the armor in place. In the garden just before His arrest, Jesus told His disciples, 'Watch and pray, that ye enter not into temptation: the spirit indeed is willing, but the flesh is weak' (Matthew 26:41)."

4. Be careful for nothing; but in every thing by prayer and supplication with thanksgiving let your requests be made known unto God. And the peace of God, which passeth all understanding, shall keep your hearts and minds through Christ Jesus. Philippians 4:6-7

5. Pray without ceasing. 1 Thessalonians 5:17

CHAPTER 8
THE FAILURE OF PRAYER

1. Complete this sentence: "The biggest reason our prayers fail is simply because we _____."

2. Aside from #1, what are the two main reasons for our failures in prayer?

3. When asked why their prayers were not answered, what was the response of most of the people who were polled?

4. In your own words, describe what is meant by this statement: "When we pray, we must make sure we are not praying to the wrong gods and not expecting eternal results from something that is temporal.

5. Complete this sentence: "When we do not see our _____ the way the Lord sees it, we forfeit the blessing of answered prayer."

ANSWERS
THE FAILURE OF PRAYER

1. The biggest reason our prayers fail is simply because we fail to pray.

2. We fail to pray right, or we fail to live right.

3. "Most people said that when their prayers were not answered, they believed it was because their prayers were not according to God's will."

4. Answers may vary, but should include the concept, "The world will pass away, so it cannot produce anything that provides lasting happiness."

5. "When we do not see our sin the way the Lord sees it, we forfeit the blessing of answered prayer."

CHAPTER 9
THE FORMULA OF PRAYER

1. "We must have pure hands when we go to the Lord in prayer." What is required for us to be clean before the Lord and to gain His ear for our prayers?

2. What often gets in the way of our willingness to confess our sins?

3. What is meant by "the need for calibration" in regard to prayer?

4. What does it mean to pray in confidence?

5. What is the simple three-part formula given for successful prayer? (Hint: the words all begin with "C.")

   _____

   _____

   _____

ANSWERS
THE FORMULA OF PRAYER

1. Honest confession is the only way to be clean before the Lord and to gain His ear for our prayers.

2. Our pride often gets in the way of our willingness to confess our sins. "The key to grace and the key to answered prayer is humility before God. Humility will naturally lead to confession."

3. "Just as a carpenter must check his work with a level and make corrections as necessary, if we want the Lord to hear and answer our prayers, then we need to align our lives with the will of God and the Word of God."

4. We can pray in confidence when we know God wants to give us what we are asking and when we know we are praying in God's will.

5. "The formula is simple: confession, calibration, and confidence."

CHAPTER 10
THE FREEDOM OF PRAYER

1. From what two things does prayer give us freedom?

2. In Philippians 4:6-7, what does God offer us when we bring our cares to Him?

3. According to Psalm 16:11, where do we find "fulness of joy"?

4. When Paul prayed for God to remove his affliction, what was God's response?

5. What did Paul mean when he said, "when I am weak, then am I strong" (2 Corinthians 12:10)?

ANSWERS
THE FREEDOM OF PRAYER

1. Prayer gives us freedom from anxiety and freedom from our own abilities.

2. Be careful for nothing; but in every thing by prayer and supplication with thanksgiving let your requests be made known unto God. And the peace of God, which passeth all understanding, shall keep your hearts and minds through Christ Jesus. Philippians 4:6-7

3. Thou wilt shew me the path of life: in thy presence is fulness of joy; at thy right hand there are pleasures for evermore. Psalm 16:11

4. And he said unto me, My grace is sufficient for thee: for my strength is made perfect in weakness. 2 Corinthians 12:9

5. "It is the realization of our weakness that causes us to stop trusting our abilities and instead to trust fully in God. When we pray and depend on Him, we are strong because He gives us His strength."

APPENDIX 2
MEMORY VERSES

The Bible has much to say about prayer, as we have seen. Here are some useful verses you can memorize.

INSTRUCTIONS ON PRAYER

- *Therefore I say unto you, What things soever ye desire, when ye pray, believe that ye receive them, and ye shall have them. Mark 11:24*

- *And he spake a parable unto them to this end, that men ought always to pray, and not to faint. Luke 18:1*

- *Be careful for nothing; but in every thing by prayer and supplication with thanksgiving let your requests be made known unto God. Philippians 4:6*

- *Continue in prayer, and watch in the same with thanksgiving; Colossians 4:2*

- *Pray without ceasing. 1 Thessalonians 5:17*

- *Humble yourselves therefore under the mighty hand of God, that he may exalt you in due time: Casting all your care upon him; for he careth for you. 1 Peter 5:6-7*

EXAMPLES OF PRAYER

- *This poor man cried, and the LORD heard him, and saved him out of all his troubles. Psalm 34:6*

- *Evening, and morning, and at noon, will I pray, and cry aloud: and he shall hear my voice. Psalm 55:17*

- *I cried unto God with my voice, even unto God with my voice; and he gave ear unto me. Psalm 77:1*

- *And in the morning, rising up a great while before day, he went out, and departed into a solitary place, and there prayed. Mark 1:35*

PROMISES OF PRAYER

· *The LORD is nigh unto all them that call upon him, to all that call upon him in truth. Psalm 145:18*

· *Call unto me, and I will answer thee, and shew thee great and mighty things, which thou knowest not. Jeremiah 33:3*

· *But thou, when thou prayest, enter into thy closet, and when thou hast shut thy door, pray to thy Father which is in secret; and thy Father which seeth in secret shall reward thee openly. Matthew 6:6*

· *Ask, and it shall be given you; seek, and ye shall find; knock, and it shall be opened unto you: For every one that asketh receiveth; and he that seeketh findeth; and to him that knocketh it shall be opened. Matthew 7:7-8*

· *Come unto me, all ye that labour and are heavy laden, and I will give you rest. Matthew 11:28*

· *And the peace of God, which passeth all understanding, shall keep your hearts and minds through Christ Jesus. Philippians 4:7*

· *And whatsoever ye shall ask in my name, that will I do, that the Father may be glorified in the Son. If ye shall ask any thing in my name, I will do it. John 14:13-14*

· *I am the vine, ye are the branches: He that abideth in me, and I in him, the same bringeth forth much fruit: for without me ye can do nothing. John 15:5*

· *He that spared not his own Son, but delivered him up for us all, how shall he not with him also freely give us all things? Romans 8:32*

- *Let us therefore come boldly unto the throne of grace, that we may obtain mercy, and find grace to help in time of need. Hebrews 4:16*

- *But he giveth more grace. Wherefore he saith, God resisteth the proud, but giveth grace unto the humble. James 4:6*

- *Draw nigh to God, and he will draw nigh to you. Cleanse your hands, ye sinners; and purify your hearts, ye double minded. James 4:8*

- *Confess your faults one to another, and pray one for another, that ye may be healed. The effectual fervent prayer of a righteous man availeth much. James 5:16*

- *Casting all your care upon him; for he careth for you. 1 Peter 5:7*

- *If we confess our sins, he is faithful and just to forgive us our sins, and to cleanse us from all unrighteousness. 1 John 1:9*

- *And whatsoever we ask, we receive of him, because we keep his commandments, and do those things that are pleasing in his sight. 1 John 3:22*

- *And this is the confidence that we have in him, that, if we ask any thing according to his will, he heareth us: And if we know that he hear us, whatsoever we ask, we know that we have the petitions that we desired of him. 1 John 5:14-15*

WARNINGS FOR PRAYER

- *If I regard iniquity in my heart, the Lord will not hear me: Psalm 66:18*

· *He that turneth away his ear from hearing the law, even his prayer shall be abomination. Proverbs 28:9*

· *Behold, the LORD'S hand is not shortened, that it cannot save; neither his ear heavy, that it cannot hear: But your iniquities have separated between you and your God, and your sins have hid his face from you, that he will not hear. Isaiah 59:1-2*

· *And when ye stand praying, forgive, if ye have ought against any: that your Father also which is in heaven may forgive you your trespasses. But if ye do not forgive, neither will your Father which is in heaven forgive your trespasses. Mark 11:25-26*

· *Watch ye and pray, lest ye enter into temptation. The spirit truly is ready, but the flesh is weak. Mark 14:38*

· *But without faith it is impossible to please him: for he that cometh to God must believe that he is, and that he is a rewarder of them that diligently seek him. Hebrews 11:6*

· *From whence come wars and fightings among you? come they not hence, even of your lusts that war in your members? Ye lust, and have not: ye kill, and desire to have, and cannot obtain: ye fight and war, yet ye have not, because ye ask not. Ye ask, and receive not, because ye ask amiss, that ye may consume it upon your lusts. Ye adulterers and adulteresses, know ye not that the friendship of the world is enmity with God? whosoever therefore will be a friend of the world is the enemy of God. James 4:1-4*

· *Likewise, ye husbands, dwell with them according to knowledge, giving honour unto the wife, as unto the weaker vessel, and as being heirs together of the grace of life; that your prayers be not hindered. 1 Peter 3:7*

Endnotes

[1] Joseph Scriven, "What a Friend We Have in Jesus," 1855.

[2] Kandi Gallaty, "How Much Do You Cherish God's Word," Facts & Trends, March 22, 2019, https://factsandtrends.net/2019/03/22/how-much-do-you-cherish-gods-word/.

[3] "Silent and Solo: How Americans Pray," Barna Group, August 15, 2017, https://www.barna.com/research/silent-solo-americans-pray.

[4] The Christian Post Reporter, "Survey: Pastors Dissatisfied With Personal Prayer Lives," May 27, 2005, https://www.christianpost.com/news/survey-pastors-dissatisfied-with-personal-prayer-lives.html.

[5] Lexico, s.v. "communion (n.)," accessed August 26, 2020, https://www.lexico.com/en/definition/communion.

[6] R. A. Torrey, How to Pray (1900; reprint, Brooklyn: G.I.L. Publications, 2018), 18.

[7] Oswald Chambers, Prayer: A Holy Occupation, ed. Harry Verploegh (Grand Rapids: Oswald Chambers Publications Association, 1992), 137.

[8] John R. Rice, Prayer: Asking and Receiving (1942; reprint, Murfreesboro: Sword of the Lord Publishers, 1979), 314.

[9] Charles H. Gabriel, "I Stand Amazed," 1905.

[10] Lewis Sperry Chafer, Major Bible Themes (1926; reprint, Grand Rapids: Zondervan Publishing House, 1971), 233.

[11] R. A. Torrey, How to Pray (1900; repr., Brooklyn: G.I.L. Publications, 2018), 18.

[12] John R. Rice, Prayer: Asking and Receiving (1942; repr., Murfreesboro: Sword of the Lord Publishers, 1979), 314.

[13] R. A. Torrey, 25.

[14] D. L. Moody, Prevailing Prayer: A Thorough Study on the Subject of Prayer, revised edition (1884; reprint, Abbotsford, WI: Aneko Press, 2018), 101.

[15] R. A. Torrey, How to Pray (1900; repr., Brooklyn: G.I.L. Publications, 2018), 54.

[16] Eliza E. Hewitt, "My Faith Has Found a Resting Place," 1891.

[17] John R. Rice, Prayer: Asking and Receiving (1942; reprint, Murfreesboro: Sword of the Lord Publishers, 1979), 167.

[18] George Mueller, Answers to Prayer, compiled by A.E.C. Brooks (Chicago: Moody Publishers, 2007), 17.

[19] R. A. Torrey, How to Pray (1900; reprint, Brooklyn: G.I.L. Publications, 2018), 85.

[20] "Martin Luther's Classic Quote on Prayer and a Busy Day," July 22, 2014, https://prayforrevival.wordpress.com/2014/07/22/martin-luthers-classic-quote-on-prayer-and-a-busy-day/.

[21] Gary Miller, "The Prayer Principle of Isolation," Talk Less Pray More! (blog), December 29, 2009, http://www.garydonmiller.com/blog/2015/3/7/the-prayer-principle-of-isolation.

[22] Vance Havner, Just a Preacher: Selected Messages from a Doctor of Souls (Chicago: Moody Publishers, 1981).

[23] R. A. Torrey, 32.

[24] R. A. Torrey, How to Pray (1900; reprint, Brooklyn: G.I.L. Publications, 2018), 30.

[25] J. H. Thayer, ed. and trans., A Greek-English Lexicon of the New Testament: Being Grimm's Wilke's Clavis Novi Testament, by Carl Grimm and Christian Wilke, corrected edition (New York, 1889), 195.

[26] Charles Spurgeon, Encouraged to Pray: Classic Sermons on Prayer (n.p.: Cross-Points Books, 2017), 29.

[27] Charles Spurgeon, 9.

[28] R. A. Torrey, 60.

[29] Charles Spurgeon, 19.

[30] Charles Spurgeon, Encouraged to Pray: Classic Sermons on Prayer (n.p.: Cross-Points Books, 2017), 192.

[31] John R. Rice, God's Cure for Anxious Care (1948; reprint, Murfreesboro: Sword of the Lord Publishers, 1976), 13.

[32] Corrie Ten Boom, Clippings from My Notebook (Nashville: Thomas Nelson, 1982), 21.

[33] Jonathan Edwards, Henry Rogers, and Sereno Edwards Dwight, The Works of Jonathan Edwards, A.M.: With an Essay on His Genius and Writings, Volume 2 (Ann Arbor, 1839).

[34] Charles Spurgeon, 210.

[35] Oswald Chambers, Prayer: A Holy Occupation, ed. Harry Verploegh (Grand Rapids: Oswald Chambers Publications Association, 1992), 7.

[36] "U.S. News and Beliefnet Prayer Survey Results," Beliefnet, Inc., accessed June 26, 2020, https://www.beliefnet.com/faiths/faith-tools/meditation/2004/12/u-s-news-beliefnet-prayer-survey-results.aspx.

[37] R. A. Torrey, How to Pray (1900; reprint, Brooklyn: G.I.L. Publications, 2018), 18.

[38] Oswald Chambers, 104.

[39] Robert Jamieson, A. R. Fausset, and David Brown, A Commentary, Critical, Experimental, and Practical, on the Old and New Testaments (London: 1871), WORDsearch Bible.

[40] Charles Spurgeon, Encouraged to Pray: Classic Sermons on Prayer (n.p.: Cross-Points Books, 2017), 178.

[41] R. A. Torrey, 35.

[42] R. A. Torrey, How to Pray (1900; reprint, Brooklyn: G.I.L. Publications, 2018), 37.

[43] R. A. Torrey, 65.

[44] D. L. Moody, Prevailing Prayer: A Thorough Study on the Subject of Prayer, rev. ed. (1884; reprint, Abbotsford, WI: Aneko Press, 2018), 79.

[45] Quoted by Auston Phelps in The Still Hour, (Boston, 1861).

[46] John R. Rice, God's Cure for Anxious Care (1948; reprint, Murfreesboro: Sword of the Lord Publishers, 1976), 61.

[47] Charles Spurgeon, Encouraged to Pray: Classic Sermons on Prayer (n.p.: Cross-Points Books, 2017), 73.

BONUS CHAPTER

The Better Life

by Joseph L. Huss

HOPE FROM PSALM 1

THE
BETTER
Life

JOSEPH L. HUSS

Dr. Joseph L. Huss
Growth Publishing Company
1300 NE 56th St., Unit 57190
Des Moines, IA 50317
www.josephhuss.com

Printed in the United States of America

Contents

1

"Often, we are prisoners
to the things we once
thought would
set us free."

What the Better Life Isn't

There's a buzz phrase that circulates within our government and our society. It is thrown about when discussing and analyzing things like safety, health, wealth, education, and geography. Governmental agencies with intelligent, well-educated people compile data and try to define it, increase it, and make it obtainable for all. This buzz phrase is *quality of life*.

One specific factor government agencies use to determine quality of life is known as the GDP – Gross Domestic Product. The GDP is "the monetary value of all the finished goods and services produced within a country's borders in a specific time period."[1] This means that quality of life is based on the value and quantity of goods and services provided to people. In other words, the more people have – the better their life. Interestingly, Robert

F. Kennedy said, "It [GDP] measures everything in short, except that which makes life worthwhile."[2] Kennedy could not be more correct; all the safety, health, wealth, education, and geography combined won't equate to a better life because the model used by the world is very different from the biblical model.

QUALITY DOESN'T MEAN ABUNDANCE

Contrary to what the secular world tells us, quality of life does not mean having an abundance of things. Sadly, even many Christians buy into this lie and fall into the trap of thinking that if they have better stuff and more stuff, they will have a better life. This is not the case. Quantity and quality of things do not necessarily equate to quality of life. The better life transcends both the quality and quantity of things. Jesus taught a parable about this subject to His disciples:

> *And he spake a parable unto them, saying, The ground of a certain rich man brought forth plentifully: And he thought within himself, saying, What shall I do, because I have no room where to bestow my fruits? And he said, This will I do: I will pull down my barns, and build greater; and there will I bestow all my fruits and my goods. And I will say to my soul, Soul, thou hast much goods laid up for many years; take thine ease, eat, drink, and be merry. But God said unto him, Thou fool, this night thy soul shall be required of thee: then whose shall those things be, which thou hast provided? **So is he that layeth up treasure for himself, and is not rich toward God.** Luke 12:16-21 (emphasis mine)*

This parable depicts the eternal fate of someone who treasures his earthly possessions, and it shows us that true quality of life isn't simply a matter of abundance. The farmer's possessions did not make his life better; they actually made his life more complex. He needed to figure out what he was going to do with all he had accumulated. One commentator put it this way: "His attitude was that he would have an easy life because he had everything he could possibly want or need."[3]

All the possessions in the world don't make life any easier. When we analyze people who have a lot of belongings, for instance, the man in the parable, we discover the stress they have over keeping and maintaining their possessions.

My mom is currently taking care of her elderly mother-in-law. She told me that they are really trying to help her, but at the same time, they are trying to help me. Through all of this, my mom has learned how important it is for them to downsize now, so I won't have to deal with an abundance of things when they die. It's tricky though. For years my mom has been trying to convince one of her children to take a certain table when she passes. She calls me every now and again about it, and this is how the conversation goes:

She says, "Honey, do you want the table?"

I reply, "No, I don't want it."

She answers bewilderedly, "It's funny that nobody wants it."

I reply, "Mom, you didn't even want it. You got it from your mother; that's why you keep wanting to hand it down. If it comes to me, it is going to Goodwill®."

She exclaims, "You wouldn't do that!"

I end the exchange with, "You won't know, will you?"

The Better Life

Having more stuff – especially a certain old table that no one really wants – has never made a better life. Ecclesiastes 4:6 says, "Better *is* an handful *with* quietness, than both the hands full *with* travail and vexation of spirit." Adam Clarke commented on this verse: "Every man who labors and amasses property is the object of envy, and is marked by the oppressor as a subject for spoil; better, therefore, to act as I do; gain little, and have little, and enjoy my handful with quietness."[4]

Generally speaking, we as a society do not want a "handful with quietness," so we work to accumulate an abundance of things. We put our value in those things, and then we spend the rest of our lives trying to protect them.

I have a collection of guns. I love my guns. For a long time, I put them under my bed. One day, my concerned, ever-practical wife asked, "What if somebody broke into the house, stole the guns, and killed someone?"

I was really convicted about this and wondered, "What do I do?" Eventually, we bought a huge gun safe. I had spent my life acquiring firearms, but I didn't have any place to put them. Now I store them in a safe to protect them from being stolen. Though I have never lost sleep over the guns, I have gone to bed thinking about what could happen if somebody broke into our house and took those firearms.

Clearly, quality of life isn't based on a person's abundance of possessions, and often we are prisoners to the things we once thought would set us free. The possessions we think will provide liberty and freedom actually create captivity. We are stuck protecting all the things we thought would give us better lives while actually reducing the quality.

The parable of the sower illustrates this point well. A sower went forth to plant seeds. He carried a basket and grabbed a handful of seeds and scattered them around. He hoped they would germinate wherever they landed. In this parable Jesus discussed four types of soil:

1. Some seeds fell by the wayside.

2. Some seeds fell on stony ground.

3. Some seeds fell among thorns.

4. Some seeds fell on good ground.

Take a look at what the seeds that fell among the thorns represented.

> He also that received seed among the thorns is he that heareth the word; and the care of this world, and the deceitfulness of riches, choke the word, and he becometh unfruitful. Matthew 13:22

This person received the Word of God, but he was deceived by riches and the cares of this world. The Word was choked out, and he became unfruitful. The desire for abundance actually kept this person from experiencing the better life.

We must change our paradigm; we must change our perspective on what quality of life means. When we equate quality with quantity, we fail. Quality of life does not mean quality and quantity of things; it means something far greater.

QUALITY DOESN'T MEAN COMFORT

Another misconception about quality of life or the better life is that it means we're going to have a comfortable life. People think that the better their lives are, the more comfortable they will become. The better life may transform an uncomfortable life into a more comfortable one, but they aren't one and the same. As a matter of fact, consider the apostles. They didn't have cozy, comfortable lives, but they each had a high quality of life.

Think of Paul and Silas in Acts 16. They cast a demon out of a possessed woman; as a result, they were beaten, thrown in jail, and "fast in the stocks" (Acts 16:24). This was not a comfortable situation. Yet, verse 25 says, "And at midnight Paul and Silas prayed, and sang praises unto God: and the prisoners heard them." Here we have two godly people in an uncomfortable situation with a high quality of life!

The better life is somewhat subjective. One person explained it this way:

> Hence, quality of life is highly subjective. Whereas one person may define quality of life according to wealth or satisfaction with life, another person may define it in terms of capabilities (e.g., having the ability to live a good life in terms of emotional and physical well-being). A disabled person may report a high quality of life, whereas a healthy person who recently lost a job may report a low quality of life.[5]

When the Apostle Paul wrote his letter to the Philippians, he was in prison awaiting trial. Yet, he had a high quality of life because he had "...the peace of God, which passeth all understanding" (Philippians 4:7a).

> *Yea doubtless, and I count all things but loss for the excellency of the knowledge of Christ Jesus my Lord: for whom I have suffered the loss of all things, and do count them but dung, that I may win Christ,*
> Philippians 3:8

As a former, well-respected religious leader, Paul had every worldly comfort. By following Jesus Christ, he lost everything. However, he valued Christ over the things from his past. We don't need a comfortable life or an abundant life to have the better life.

Solomon said in Ecclesiastes 2:9-11, "So I was great, and increased more than all that were before me in Jerusalem: also my wisdom remained with me. And whatsoever mine eyes desired I kept not from them, I withheld not my heart from any joy; for my heart rejoiced in all my labour: and this was my portion of all my labour. Then I looked on all the works that my hands had wrought, and on the labour that I had laboured to do: and, behold, all *was* vanity and vexation of spirit, and *there was* no profit under the sun."

The Apostle Paul reflected on his life and said, "I lost all things, but it was only dung compared to what I have in Christ." Yet, Solomon said, "I had everything my heart desired," but his life was empty. Why? Because quality of life doesn't come from a comfortable life. We will experience some discomfort in our lives and have struggles, trials, and problems. We are promised that in 2 Timothy 3:12: "Yea, and all that will live godly in Christ Jesus shall suffer persecution."

The better life will not always be a bed of roses. When we become Christians and start to serve the Lord, not everything will be problem free. If we were to ask the apostles if they had better lives after trusting Christ, forsaking all, and following Him, every single one of them would say, "Yes, I had a much better life!"

Tradition holds that the Apostles died in the following manner: Matthew suffered martyrdom by being slain with a sword at a distant city of Ethiopia. Mark expired at Alexandria, after being cruelly dragged through the streets of that city. Luke was hanged upon an olive tree in the classic land of Greece. John was put in a caldron of boiling oil, but escaped death in a miraculous manner, and was afterward banished to Patmos. Peter was crucified at Rome with his head downward. James, the Greater, was beheaded at Jerusalem. James, the Less, was thrown from a lofty pinnacle of the temple, and then beaten to death with a fuller's club. Bartholomew was flayed alive. Andrew was bound to a cross, whence he preached to his persecutors until he died. Thomas was run through the body with a lance at Coromandel in the East Indies. Jude was shot to death with arrows. Matthias was first stoned and then beheaded. Barnabas of the Gentiles was stoned to death at Salonica. Paul, after various tortures and persecutions, was at length beheaded at Rome by the Emperor Nero.[6]

Even though they lost all things, suffered persecution, and were killed, every single one of them would say that they had a better life because the better life means a life with Christ, not a comfortable one.

Martin Luther King, Jr. said, "The quality, not the longevity, of one's life, is what is important."[7] What will we base the quality of our lives on? The quantity of our things? Being comfortable? If we do, we will struggle. We will battle to find the peace of God in our lives because the better life doesn't come from abundance or comfort.

If the better life isn't found in comfort or abundance, where is it found? It begins when someone places their faith in Christ alone for salvation. The Bible describes our lives before we believe the gospel as "dead in trespasses and sins" (Ephesians 2:1b). In this position we can't experience the better life because God's wrath is abiding on us.

> *He that believeth on the Son hath everlasting life: and he that believeth not the Son shall not see life; but the wrath of God abideth on him. John 3:36*

God's wrath abides on us because of our sin. Heaven is a perfect place, so we cannot enter Heaven if we have sin. Unfortunately, we all have sin.

> *For all have sinned, and come short of the glory of God; Romans 3:23*

Because of our sin, we have earned death, but God offers us eternity in Heaven as a gift.

> *For the wages of sin is death; but the gift of God is eternal life through Jesus Christ our Lord. Romans 6:23*

He is able to offer us forgiveness for our sins and eternity in Heaven because He paid the price for our sins when He died on the cross.

> *All we like sheep have gone astray; we have turned every one to his own way; and the LORD hath laid on him the iniquity of us all. Isaiah 53:6*

The Better Life

> *For he [God the Father] hath made him [Jesus Christ]*
> *to be sin for us, who knew no sin; that we might be*
> *made the righteousness of God in him.*
> *2 Corinthians 5:21*

He shed His blood on the cross and paid the penalty that we deserved, but that is not where the story ends. Three days later He arose!

> *For I delivered unto you first of all that which I also*
> *received, how that Christ died for our sins according*
> *to the scriptures; And that he was buried, and that he*
> *rose again the third day according to the scriptures:*
> *1 Corinthians 15:3-4*

His death and resurrection were sufficient to save us. We must trust in Christ alone for salvation. The only way of salvation is through the sacrifice of our Savior – not by anything that we do.

> *For by grace are ye saved through faith; and that not of*
> *yourselves: it is the gift of God: Not of works, lest any*
> *man should boast. Ephesians 2:8-9*

Once we trust Christ to save us, He gives us everlasting life. Because of this gift, we can know for sure that we are going to Heaven.

> *For God so loved the world, that he gave his only*
> *begotten Son, that whosoever believeth in him should*
> *not perish, but have everlasting life. John 3:16*

> *These things have I written unto you that believe on*
> *the name of the Son of God; that ye may know that ye*

have eternal life, and that ye may believe on the name of the Son of God. 1 John 5:13

Trust Christ as your Savior, and you will have the promise of eternal life. This is the first and most important step to experience *The Better Life*.

Endnotes

[1] Will Kenton, "Gross Domestic Product – GDP," 2018, investopedia.com/terms/g/gdp.asp

[2] Robert F. Kennedy, Remarks at the University of Kansas, March 18, 1968, jfklibrary.org/learn/about-jfk/the-kennedyfam ily/robert-f-kennedy/robert-f-kennedy-speeches/remarks-at-the-university-of-kansas-march-18-1968

[3] John F. Walvoord and Roy B. Zuck, *The Bible Knowledge Commentary*, Luke 12:13-21, Victor Books, 1983

[4] Adam Clarke, *Adam Clarke's Commentary*, Ecclesiastes 4:6, 1831

[5] Crispen Jenkinson, "Quality of Life," Encyclopedia Britannica, Inc., 2019, britannica.com/topic/quality-of-life

[6] John Berstecher, "Apostles as Martyrs," 2019, sermonillustra tions.com/a-z/a/apostles.htm

[7] Martin Luther King, Jr., brainyquote.com/quotes/martin_lu ther_king_jr_297515

The Better Life
is available
on Amazon.

ACKNOWLEDGEMENTS

I want to express my sincere gratitude to all who have made this book possible. I want to thank Joel and Lydia Collison for doing amazing work on the front end – transcribing, editing, and proofing this book. I would also like to thank David Coon, who has done several books for me: he is, indeed, a fantastic editor.

Most importantly, I would like to thank my dear wife, Dana! She has not only been the exact help meet that God wanted me to have, but she is also an amazing inspiration in my life. She has helped me all along the way with the editing, proofing, and design of this book. But she has done so much more than that! She has prayed with me – she has prayed for me – and she has become, at many times, the center of my prayers! I love you, Dana. I'm so thankful that the Lord answered my prayer and brought you into my life.

Made in the USA
Coppell, TX
14 January 2024